CAMBRIDGE LIBRARY COLLECTION

Books of enduring scholarly value

History

The books reissued in this series include accounts of historical events and movements by eye-witnesses and contemporaries, as well as landmark studies that assembled significant source materials or developed new historiographical methods. The series includes work in social, political and military history on a wide range of periods and regions, giving modern scholars ready access to influential publications of the past.

The Present Position and Prospects of the British Trade with China

James Matheson (1796–1878) became a leading taipan, with significant influence and power in Hong Kong. When this pamphlet was published, in 1836, he was still trading from Canton (Guangzhou) and, following the abolition of the East India Company's monopoly on trade with China, appealed to the British government to pressure the Chinese to lift the severe restrictions on trading. He suggests that despite the efforts of the merchants, China refuses to acknowledge the law of nations, to trade fairly, and as such has 'long since surrendered her rights and is no longer in a position to enforce them'. Matheson's personal appeal to the Duke of Wellington was rebuffed, but his business partner, William Jardine, later persuaded Lord Palmerston to adopt a tougher approach, which ultimately led to the First Opium War. This is a powerful and provocative text: a defence of both free trade and an aggressive foreign policy.

Cambridge University Press has long been a pioneer in the reissuing of out-of-print titles from its own backlist, producing digital reprints of books that are still sought after by scholars and students but could not be reprinted economically using traditional technology. The Cambridge Library Collection extends this activity to a wider range of books which are still of importance to researchers and professionals, either for the source material they contain, or as landmarks in the history of their academic discipline.

Drawing from the world-renowned collections in the Cambridge University Library and other partner libraries, and guided by the advice of experts in each subject area, Cambridge University Press is using state-of-the-art scanning machines in its own Printing House to capture the content of each book selected for inclusion. The files are processed to give a consistently clear, crisp image, and the books finished to the high quality standard for which the Press is recognised around the world. The latest print-on-demand technology ensures that the books will remain available indefinitely, and that orders for single or multiple copies can quickly be supplied.

The Cambridge Library Collection brings back to life books of enduring scholarly value (including out-of-copyright works originally issued by other publishers) across a wide range of disciplines in the humanities and social sciences and in science and technology.

The Present Position and Prospects of the British Trade with China

James Matheson

CAMBRIDGE
UNIVERSITY PRESS

CAMBRIDGE UNIVERSITY PRESS

Cambridge, New York, Melbourne, Madrid, Cape Town,
Singapore, São Paolo, Delhi, Mexico City

Published in the United States of America by Cambridge University Press, New York

www.cambridge.org
Information on this title: www.cambridge.org/9781108045896

© in this compilation Cambridge University Press 2012

This edition first published 1836
This digitally printed version 2012

ISBN 978-1-108-04589-6 Paperback

THE

PRESENT POSITION AND PROSPECTS

OF THE

BRITISH TRADE WITH CHINA;

TOGETHER WITH

AN OUTLINE OF SOME LEADING OCCURRENCES

IN

ITS PAST HISTORY.

———

By JAMES MATHESON, Esq.

OF THE FIRM OF JARDINE, MATHESON AND CO, OF CANTON.

———

LONDON:

SMITH, ELDER AND CO., CORNHILL,

BOOKSELLERS TO THEIR MAJESTIES.

———

1836.

LONDON :
PRINTED BY STEWART AND CO.,
OLD BAILEY.

ADVERTISEMENT.

THE author of the ensuing pages has been engaged in active commercial pursuits at Canton for the last seventeen years.

He has spared no pains to present a faithful and popular view of that most important subject, the British trade with China. For this purpose he has not only referred to every source of authentic information, but has been enabled to avail himself of the assistance of a distinguished friend particularly conversant with the subject of international law.

He has occasionally adopted the felicitous language of his admirable friend Mr. Holman, to the accuracy of whose observations he is glad to have this opportunity of bearing testimony.

9, *Hanover Street, Hanover Square,*
February, 1836.

CONTENTS.

PRESENT POSITION,

&c. &c.

It has pleased Providence to assign to the Chinese,—a people characterised by a marvellous degree of imbecility, avarice, conceit, and obstinacy,—the possession of a vast portion of the most desirable parts of the earth, and a population estimated as amounting to nearly a third of the whole human race. It has been the policy of this extraordinary people, to shroud themselves, and all belonging to them, in mystery impenetrable,—to monopolize all the advantages of their situation. They consequently exhibit a spirit of *exclusiveness* on a grand scale. From what this has resulted,—whether from conceit, or selfishness, or from a consciousness that the ancient but feeble framework of their political system cannot bear the rude concussions of modern times,—the too near inspection of inquisitive and ambitious fellow-nations, it matters not here to inquire. Such is the fact; and the result is that China remains, at this moment, " a boundless field of indefinite curiosity and vague speculation." " It is one of

B

their principal maxims," observes Mr. Auber, "and one which they believe contributes most to good government, not to suffer foreigners to settle in the empire : for besides their contempt for other nations, whom they look upon as barbarous, they are persuaded that a difference of people would introduce among them a diversity of manner and customs, which, by little and little, would bring on personal quarrels, and these would end in parties, and proceed to rebellions, fatal to the tranquillity of their empire."* These notions are carried to a surprising extent. They permit to Europeans no intercourse but of a commercial character, and that only of the scantiest and most ungracious description,—restricted to the veriest outposts and confines of the empire. " Foreign trade receives no support from the government; it is barely tolerated: for it is always at variance with that jealous policy which draws a line of perpetual demarkation between China and the rest of the world."† On no earthly consideration will they permit a "*barbarian*" footstep to transgress the limits of Canton, almost the southernmost extre-

---

* Auber on British and Foreign Intercourse with China, p. 56.

† Encyclop. Metropolit. part xiii.—See, however, the Second Appendix to the Third Report of the Select Committee of the House of Commons on the Affairs of the East India Company, p. 527.

mity of the empire, fifteen hundred miles from
the capital; and in the pursuit of their commercial avocations at that place, foreigners are
constantly exposed to the most ignominious
surveillance and restrictions.

Studiously and obstinately presenting this
repulsive aspect, discouraging all attempts to
become acquainted with her national character,
it is not to be wondered at that distant nations,
if ever their curiosity had been excited concerning China, suffered it at length to die away
into a feeling of contemptuous indifference : and
China, its position, customs, and inhabitants,
came, at length, to be spoken of much in the
same spirit as one would speculate concerning
the suppositious tenants of the moon. It was
reserved, however, for those " princes of the
earth"—the MERCHANTS—to overcome these
feelings of indifference or repugnance. A spirit
of noble and persevering enterprise led them to
dare all dangers, to despise all difficulties. They
soon perceived how vast a field China afforded
for commerce, even under the most discouraging
circumstances ; and after many years of persevering struggle, they succeeded in opening a
communication between Europe and China,
which has led to an annual interchange of
millions of capital. The history of the British
intercourse with China during a period of
nearly two centuries, is indeed an unparalleled

one, It is fraught with instruction, and now is the auspicious moment for turning it to account.

It is melancholy, but no ways surprising, to reflect upon the extent to which ignorance and misapprehension as to the nature of our commercial intercourse with China prevail in this country. The reason above assigned will, in some measure, account for it; especially when added to a consideration of the disheartening difficulties attending the attempt to acquire a knowledge of the Chinese language; the prodigious distance of China; the exclusively mercantile character of our intercourse, (naturally destitute of interesting and stirring topics)—and that, too, hitherto committed to the exclusive keeping of the East India Company; who never manifested any particular readiness to admit the public to a knowledge of the mysteries of Leadenhall-street, but, on the contrary, rather acquiesced in, and encouraged the notion of the unprepossessing nature of such inquiries. It may be safely asserted that four-fifths of our fellow-countrymen know, or care to know, little more about our relations with China, than that the delightful beverage " which cheers but not inebriates," and a few articles of ornamental dress and curious earthenware annually find their way hither from that mysterious and remote region. They trouble not themselves to inquire or think about the intense anxieties, sufferings, and dangers of their enterprising fellow-countrymen, by whose means these articles are transmitted; they feel little or no interest in being told that some of the most respectable of their fellow-countrymen are daily subjected to injuries and insults not merely of a harassing, but even of a horrible description,* while in the prosecution of honourable and responsible undertakings; that the vast and lucrative trade between Great Britain and China, with all its extensive dependencies both at home and abroad, is liable to be, and frequently has been, suspended on the most frivolous and ridiculous pretences that could be devised by the capricious and unprincipled local authorities of Canton; that the British nation and its sovereign, are constantly and openly characterised by the Chinese in their official edicts in the grossest terms of contempt and dishonour; that our unoffending representative, Lord Napier, who travelled to China at the instance of the Chinese government itself, no sooner reached the Canton river, than he encountered such indignities and injuries as speedily destroyed him—the whole trade being

---

* See the atrocious " *proclamation against the Hong merchants conniving at and abetting vice in foreigners,*" issued annually by the Governor and Hoppo.

at the same time, abruptly and ruinously suspended for upwards of a month ; that our sovereign and his people, in short, were treated with
such disdain, and visited with such injuries, as
they have never hitherto experienced, or chosen
to endure. These latter topics certainly excited,
from their singularity and the suddenness of
their communication, a few days' notice ; they
then disappeared from the daily journals, and
all seems now utterly forgotten,—as though the
gravest questions of commercial interest, and
even of the national honour, had not been intimately involved in, if not compromised by them!
The abolition of the East India Company's charter,—a great political measure,—pregnant as it
was with prodigious consequences, made a certain stir while under parliamentary discussion ;
the national spirit seemed kindled for a moment
against so unjust a monopoly as that enjoyed by
the company in question. It disappeared,—the
public was satisfied, and its attention and energies
were forthwith directed to fresh objects. How
the breaking up of the old, and the introduction
of the new system of commercial intercourse,
would be received in China—*how it would work,*
—whether any and what further alterations
would be rendered necessary, are questions that
seem by tacit and universal consent to have
been left to the few individuals who from interest or inclination concern themselves with the

subject. This great and decisive measure, highly beneficial as its consequences are calculated to prove to our commercial intercourse with China, has nevertheless been attended with effects, some of them, perhaps, not wholly unforeseen, and some of them unexpectedly unfortunate; such as imperiously call upon the government for a prompt interference,—a vigorous superintendence in reconstructing the system of our commercial intercourse with China. With the government, indeed, it rests at this moment to say, in effect, whether the British trade with China shall any longer continue; whether our merchants shall be enabled to carry it on any longer, either with safety and honour to themselves, or their country. It has wisely thought fit to substitute *individual* for *corporate* enterprise in trading to China. Surely, then, it is called upon not to desert the new system in its birth, but to protect and foster it; to compensate for the withdrawal of that "local habitation and a name,"—that local influence and power which have hitherto (however imperfectly) sheltered and protected our interests in China,—by such demonstrations as shall convince the people of that country, that our individual not less than our corporate traders, enjoy the full countenance and support of the British government.

That this vitally-important subject may be

easily and at the same time thoroughly understood, it has been thought advisable to give a
short and popular sketch of the present position
and prospects of Anglo-Chinese affairs,—the
sources of the existing evils, and the means by
which they may be remedied, and the trade,
so important in every point of view to this country, placed on a permanent and advantageous
footing.

However skilful and successful may have
been deemed, in some respects, the East India
Company's long administration of Chinese commercial affairs, it is impossible for any one to
peruse with attention the authentic records of
their proceedings, without perceiving that their
policy, even if not altogether based upon fundamental errors, has exhibited many features of
a most short-sighted and mischievous character;
that the ill effects of many of their measures exist at this moment, and oppose most formidable
barriers to the progress of their successors. It
may be questionable whether the East India
Company, in their anxiety to secure their commercial interests, have not, for a long series of
years, made sacrifices that were inconsistent not
only with the honour of the British nation, but
with its permanent interests, even in a commercial point of view. It is very grievous and
humiliating to reflect that our present degradation in the eyes of China, and the ruinous

exactions she inflicts upon us, are, in reality,
self-imposed; that—

> " The thorns which we have reaped, are of the tree
> We planted. They have torn us, and we bleed."

Without tracing out their whole administration,
it may be stated, that many of their most important measures are based upon an utter ignorance
of the real character of the Chinese,—such as
one could scarcely have supposed possible, after
so many years' intimate experience. In the
year 1751, for instance, the Court of Directors,
finding the trade suffering from continual impositions, authorized the supercargoes to *bribe the
local authorities*,* in order to obtain a discontinuance of such exactions. Could they have
taken a step more destructive to their own interests? Had they not already had experience,
year after year, of the mercenary and rapacious
character of the Chinese?—What, then, were
the consequences, and who could not, if possessed of but ordinary forethought, have antici-
pated them? Six years afterwards we find the
bribed authorities of Canton expending their
gains in bribery at the court of Pekin, *and
thereby securing a monopoly of the whole foreign
trade!* The immediate consequence was our
exclusion from trading at any of the other ports
to which we had, till then, been accustomed

---

* Auber, 167.

to resort: and thus we lost the only mode we had of holding the Canton authorities in check— our only rod *in terrorem* over them, namely, the threat—always effectual, of removing our trade to such other ports! One circumstance will suffice to show the nature of the powers we have lost. In the year 1721, the officers of the Honourable Company's Ship, *Cadogan*, while quietly walking in the street at Canton, were seized by one of the Canton authorities, on account of the accidental death of the Hoppo's officer. "A strong representation was made by the supercargoes to the Hoppo. They stated that unless immediate redress was afforded, they should recommend the Company to remove their commercial dealings from Canton to some other port. The determination evinced by the supercargoes, and the apprehension of the local authorities that they might lose the trade, produced a good effect. The mandarin who committed the affront was degraded from his office, and a promise was given that he should be bambooed, and rendered incapable of again serving the Emperor."* From the moment of taking this false step, may be dated the commencement of a long series of intolerable oppression and insult. Ignorant of the obvious consequences of the ill-advised measure in

---

* Auber, pp. 155-6.

question,—of the all but irresponsible authority
of the unprincipled local authorities at Canton,
and the impossibility of appealing from them, or
gaining any kind of access to the Court at Pekin,—of the far-sighted cunning and inflexible
pertinacity of the Chinese character,—we flung
ourselves, as it were, bound hand and foot into
their power. In vain have we from that period
to the present, reiterated our complaints, as imposition and insult assumed new and more galling
features. We have been either trifled with by
delusive promises, or repulsed with mockery
and threats of an aggravation of our injuries.
In answer to our feeble complaints, they shake
their heads, and coolly remark,—" If the foreigners dislike our restrictions,* as difficult to
be endured, it is perfectly competent to them
not to take the trouble to come so great a distance!" Again, the Hoppo in 1831 :† "Lately,
the English merchants have presented a petition
stating that the whole scope of the regulations
is at variance with the requisitions of justice—
thus whining, disputing, and contradicting, and
also requesting to appeal to the Emperor, not to
permit their being put in practice. This is extreme insolence and opposition. If the said private merchants really regard their property,
they ought indeed to trade on as usual : but if

---

* Auber, 332.   † Auber, 356-7.

they dislike the restraints imposed by the orders of Government, and consider their own private affairs to be disadvantageous, they may entirely withdraw from the trade, and not trouble themselves to come from a great distance, through many countries of different languages."—The tone and spirit of these recent edicts, are worthy of particular notice.

Another fatal and fundamental error discoverable in the administration of the East India Company, has been its uniform,—its anxiously pacific and submissive policy towards the Chinese. In their excessive eagerness to secure their trade, they have been led, from time to time, into making the most humiliating and dangerous concessions, acquiescing in pretensions on the part of the Chinese which were alike inconsistent with individual and national honour: the natural consequence of which was to place themselves in an abject and degraded position, in the eyes of the Chinese, which could not do otherwise than invite additional insult and exaction. When the Court of Directors have been pressed by their Canton representatives, whose dispatches constantly detailed the infliction of the grossest insults and impositions, and contained vehement expostulations on account of their dogged adherence to an acquiescent and submissive line of policy,—cogently representing, at the same time, the numerous instances in

which vigorous and decisive measures had been
attended with complete success,—how did the
Court receive them, and reply? At one time
by a peremptory mandate for the dismissal and
return home of the spirited Select Committee;
at another by rebuking their intolerance of insult and injury,—invariably, by the recommenda-
tion of " mild and pacific measures, demeanor,
and conduct:" and all this on the plea of the capital importance of preserving our trade. They
were sternly reminded that " our intercourse
with China was exclusively of a *commercial* character"—and, in effect, that we ought therefore
not to resent treatment otherwise inconsistent
with the national honour. In January 1832, for
instance, the Directors, writing to the Select
Committee, in consequence of their representations of many very serious transactions, vitally affecting the honour and interests of this country,
observe—

" The commerce between Great Britain and
China is too important to be put to hazard without the most urgent and imperious necessity,
and on no account, upon considerations of a
personal nature. It is of essential moment to
the Indian as well as to the home revenues,
both as regards the State and the East India
Company, as well as in the regular supply to
the British public of an article of general con-
sumption. We sought that trade originally: the

advantages which it has yielded have induced us to exert every endeavour to secure its continuance.* The preservation of the national honour, is in the hands of His Majesty's Government; and it must be for the King's Ministers alone to take the responsibility of deciding upon the adoption of extreme measures for vindicating that honour, if insulted. These measures, if resorted to, will most materially affect the valuable interests at present dependent upon a peaceful prosecution of our intercourse with China." Is it not clear from the spirit and tone of this dispatch, and many similar ones,—enjoining " endurance" for " commerce' sake" up to the point of " *some urgent and imperious necessity,*"—that it amounted to a virtual and practical prohibition of remonstrance or resistance, on *any* ground? Is it likely that in the face of such dispatches the Select Committee would have ventured to incur such immense responsibilities as those shadowed out by the Directors? Surely the concluding paragraph is, in every sense, an unworthy one! How vague and cold the allusion to the province of " His Majesty's Government"—and even *their* interference in vindication of the national honour, represented as " most materially affecting the valuable interests of trade!" Can there be a more artful or effectual way of conveying,

---

* Auber, 358-9.   See also *id*. pp. 281-2.

without seeming to do so, their real wishes,—*i. e.*
that in no case should resistance be attempted,
let the Chinese do what they would? Without
being anxious to fasten ungenerous imputations
upon the Directors of the East India Company,
one cannot help entertaining a suspicion that this
line of policy was dictated by a desire to fix the
Company firmly in the favour of the Chinese,
and render them reluctant to trade with Great
Britain through any other medium than one so
supple, so acquiescent, so " peaceable !"*

This truculent, vain-glorious people have been
pleased to consider all other inhabitants of the
earth (as already intimated) as BARBARIANS,—
destitute of all pretensions to civil, political, or
moral excellence. They will not permit themselves to be polluted by these " barbarians" in-
termingling with them,—except to such an extent and in such a manner as affords them opportunity for extracting from them a great revenue, by means of the most unblushing
extortion.

" If an European commit any breach of the
laws, he is not taken before a magistrate to

---

* Mr. Auber quotes from the " Report on China Trade"—
(Parliamentary Papers, &c.) with an air of triumph, that the
East India Company have been able " to *temporize* with the
Chinese, without loss of character !"—p. 398.

answer for his conduct; but is subjected to personal violence from mere underlings, or has his Chinese servants taken away or imprisoned, and his provisions stopped, till he submit to an arbitrary mulct; which, on his refusal to pay, is exacted from the Hong merchant with whom he may chance to have most dealings; and this Hong merchant again, is imprisoned and his trade stopped until he make good the arbitrary demand,—the European never having a trial, or an opportunity of justifying himself!

"In like manner, an European has no access to a magistrate or government functionary, to claim redress for any outrage to which he may have been subjected, — overcharge of duties, stoppage of trade, or other grievance, but must appeal through the Hong merchants, who are commonly the authors of the grievances suffered, and who are able to tell their own story to the Mandarin, without any countervailing statement from the European. The Hong merchants, in short, ten or twelve in number, besides possessing a monopoly of all European trade, are vested with authority to govern Europeans, ' who' (to use the words of a Government edict) ' must not be allowed of their own accord to go out and into their dwellings, lest they should trade and carry on clandestine transactions with traitorous natives.' Nor after the departure of their ships are they allowed to remain in Canton city, *to find out the prices of goods,* to make purchases, and acquire profit."

The only terms on which they will suffer a commercial intercourse to be carried on with the frontiers, are an implicit acknowledgment of its springing from the " amazing and unmerited condescension" of the Emperor of China towards " his reverently-submissive tributary" the King of England, and his " barbarian and profligate subjects." It is true, that a few attempts have been made to shake off such a badge of ignominious servitude,—feeble, however, and few : the occasions on which such manifestations have been made, have been, too often, indiscreetly selected, and the ultimate results correspondingly unfortunate. Of what avail were a few momentary flashes of indignation and independence, in the midst of a long and dark interval of acquiescence and submission? The Chinese came at length to treat such exhibitions as really but the spasms of weakness, however momentarily formidable—as indications of the real extent of their power over us. Listen to the language in which the Company's supercargoes are characterized by the Viceroy of Canton : " *Good principles and solemn truths have no effect upon them ; and I was compelled to intercept their trade—to touch their gains; and no sooner was that done, than they submitted. They are a mercenary gain-scheming set of adventurers, whom reason cannot rule. The*

c

dread of not making money is that which alone influences them."*

" It will have been apparent," says even Mr. Auber, speaking of the year 1791—" from the detail already given, that the Chinese, instead of relaxing in their conduct towards the English, since their first intercourse with Canton, in consequence of the increased value of their commerce, and the length of their connexion with China, only inflicted additional impositions on the trade, and,—as the supercargoes justly stated,—acted as if they *'were aware that the importance we attached to its continuance induced us to submit to almost every kind of indignity.'"*†*

If such were the contemptuous opinion entertained and expressed concerning us by the Chinese in 1791,—the legitimate result of a series of timorous submissions on our part,—how must we reckon upon that opinion being *now* strengthened! During the long period of our intercourse, how many have been the indignities we have either tamely submitted to, or—far worse—feebly and ineffectually resisted!—how many unwise compromises have taken place — how much of individual and national insult — what an extent of injury to our commercial interests

---

* Dr. Morrison's Notices concerning China.—Introd. pp. 6-7. Buonaparte, also, characterised us as a nation of shopkeepers !

† Auber, 192.

have been inflicted, on pretences equally absurd! The vaunting tone assumed by the
Chinese when speaking of the foreign trade,—
repeatedly asserting it to be a matter of utter
insignificance,—that " the celestial empire
views them as really not of the importance of a
fibre or particle of dust,"* has been fearfully and
implicitly listened to, and credited by the East
India Company, and been ever present as a
bugbear at all their consultations at Leadenhall
Street, influencing them to repel all the indig-
nant expostulations of their representatives at
Canton, and sternly enjoin upon them the
necessity of " submission for the trade's sake,"
—lest " the interests of the Company's trade
should suffer!" Vain, short-sighted, and ruinous policy! Not perceiving that the dreaded
cause of future mischief, was really only the effect of their own former, and continuing miscon-
duct and erroneous policy! Had they but paid
a just deference to the judgment of those whose
local opportunities and experience had qualified
them to form a sound judgment upon the matter,
they would, long—long ago, have learnt that—
" submission to insult has shewn the Chinese how
valuable is the trade, and they have acted accordingly, in too many instances, in interrupting and
annoying it,—and hence, perhaps, has originated

---

* Viceroy's Edict. 25th January, 1830,—Auber, 326.

*the erroneous supposition that to them the trade is
a matter of indifference."** Hear again, the re-
proachful and contemptuous language of the
Hoppo Chung in reply to the Committee's letter
of October 28th, 1830, as affording melancholy
evidence of the results of long-continued submission to Chinese outrage. The Committee
had complained bitterly of a proclamation—
(already hinted at)—of a most revolting nature,
annually stuck against their factory, and requested its removal :—

" In the petition they say that the insulting
proclamation, suspended against the Company's
Hong, has been reluctantly borne with for many
years, by foreign merchants. . . *It has been stuck
up against the Company's Hong for more than
thirty years.* It did not commence to-day. As
they say the language of the proclamation was
rather ignominious,—*why did not the former barbarian merchants early indulge their anger*, and
with hearts dead to the subject, cease to come
again to knock-head at the service for an open
market? Why did they cross an immense
ocean, through numerous dangers, and every
year come?"†

" The intercourse of foreign nations with the
Chinese," says Holman, " is carried on under

---

* Extract, China Consult. 7th Oct. 1830, — 2d Appendix to the 3d Report of the Select Committee of the House
of Commons, p. 457.

† 2d Appendix to the 3d Report, &c. p. 427.

every disadvantage which their ignorant pride
and vain confidence in their own resources, can
suggest. But the readiness with which they
yield to every strenuous opposition to their exclusive measures, while it points out the weakness of their character, affords a convincing
proof of the prejudicial consequence of too
pliant a submission to their jealous regulations.
Foreigners, whom they entitle *Barbarians,* are
invariably treated as inferiors; and the lowest
of the people are incited, by the language and
representations of their governors, to conduct
themselves with insolence, and even violence."*
—One cannot help here pausing to notice how
noble a contrast to this conduct has been and is
still exhibited by the English nation! "Montes-
quieu," says Blackstone, "remarks with a degree of admiration, that the English have made
the protection of foreign merchants one of the
articles of their national liberties ; it being provided by Magna Charta, that all foreign merchants, unless publicly prohibited beforehand,
shall have safe conduct to depart from, to come
into, to tarry in, and to go through England for
the exercise of merchandize,—without any unreasonable imposts, except in time of war."†—
But to return—

---

* Holman's Voy. and Trav. 245.

† The merchants of the Hanse towns, established in London, enjoyed various privileges and immunities; they were

The two co-operating causes above generally alluded to, have produced results of a most unfortunate description: and now,—at the very moment when the British trade is placed upon a new footing,—our merchants find themselves in the most precarious and defenceless position with reference not only to their commercial interests, but even their personal safety,—that was ever yet witnessed in China. The Chinese have indeed profited by their long experience,— their successful practices upon our credulity and imbecility; and the advantages accruing to them are of far too solid a description to be now

---

permitted to govern themselves by their own laws and regulations; the custody of one of the gates of the city (Bishopsgate) was committed to their care; and the duties on various sorts of imported commodities were considerably reduced in their favour. In 1474, the King assigned to them in absolute property, a large space of ground, with the buildings upon it, in Thames-street, now denominated the Steel-yard. It was further stipulated, that they should not be subject to the judges of the English Admiralty Court; also that the privileges awarded to them should be published, as often as they judged proper, in all the sea-port towns of England. These privileges were not wholly abolished till the year 1597.—*M'Culloch's Commercial Dictionary*, p. 623.

In Turkey and some other countries characterized by an imperfect state of civilization, such as then prevailed in England, and still does in China, immunities nearly similar are enjoyed by foreign traders even at the present day. The Chinese alone seem to enjoy, as a monopoly, the undisputed power of persecuting and maltreating foreign merchants.

lightly parted with. They will calculate, and reasonably enough, upon a *continuance* of our forbearance. They will make us feel, at every point,—in every transaction, social and commercial—our abject dependence upon their sovereign will and pleasure. Our position was fearful enough in 1780,—when the Company's Supercargoes thus wrote to the Directors:— " Foreigners are not here allowed the benefit of the Chinese law, nor have they privileges in common with the nation. They are governed merely by such rules as the mandarins for the time being declare to be their will; and the reason why so few inconveniences happen, from irregularities, is, that the officers of the Government, on such occasions, rather choose to exact money from the security merchants, compradors, &c. than use rigorous measures from which they gain nothing. Their corruption, therefore, is the foreigner's security." Again, on the 23d February, 1815, the President of the Select Committee at Canton thus writes to the Chairman of the Court of Directors:—" There is in fact no charge, of whatever nature it may be, whether of treason against the state, or a violation of the laws and regulations of the Empire, that Chunqua may not procure to be alleged against any member of the Committee ; and with the same facility, by means of the bamboo or torture, any number of witnesses may be brought forward to attest the truth of the accusation."* In another communication, in the same year, the Select Committee " offer further melancholy proof *of the total and entire absence of truth, justice, or mercy from Chinese tribunals:* and where the undue influence of money is applied, all chance of a fair trial ceases to the unfortunate person accused."†

If such were the state of matters in 1780 and 1815, when the potent influence of the East India Company existed in its plenitude at Canton, what may we not prepare to expect at the present time, when the local influence of Great Britain is withdrawn? Let those who are disposed to answer such a question lightly, reflect upon the disastrous issue of the mission of Lord Napier!

That our intercourse with China has continued in a comparatively prosperous condition, under the management of the East India Company, is attributable solely to the judgment and firmness *occasionally* displayed by the resident representatives of the Company: but it is truly painful to observe the reception which the intelligence of their conduct invariably met with at Leadenhall Street.‡ They, whose local know-

---

* 2d Appendix to the 3d Report, &c. p. 502.

† Extract Letter in the Secret Department, &c. 16th Jan. 1815.—2d Append. &c. 528.

‡ See particularly the bitter complaint of the Select Committee at Canton to the Directors, 18th November, 1816. Second Appendix, &c. pp. 531—5.

ledge and long experience surely best qualified them for dealing successfully with the Chinese, and effectually serving our interests, are found to be most strenuous and incessant in their recommendations of a firm and resolute tone and bearing being assumed by this country, in resisting similar demonstrations on the part of the Chinese. Whatever may have been their inclinations and prepossessions previous to acquiring a thorough knowledge of the subject, they no sooner had an opportunity of acquiring a practical insight into the character and conduct of the Chinese, than we find them earnestly expostulating with the home authorities on their constant inculcation of submission and acquiescence. It may be instructive to detail a few instances, out of a very great number, that are on record.

On the 22d February, 1814, the Select Committee remark—

" Carrying on an extensive commerce, sufficient to excite the rapacity of the officers of Government, protected by no laws, but on the contrary subject to such regulations as are made so vague and undefined, as to admit of any interference or interpretation that a corrupt or despotic government may be disposed to give them,—our only hope of preventing the recurrence of these attacks is by a firm and decided resistance." *

---

* Second Appendix, &c. p. 487.

On the 4th December, in the same year:—

" From the experience and knowledge we possess of the government, we are satisfied that their conviction that their injustice will not be submitted to, is the only security we can possess for these attempts being discontinued." *

On the 6th February, 1815:—

"Your honourable Committee will no doubt appreciate the difficulties and anxieties that must attend our differences and discussions with this Government. We feel, however, that they are unavoidable; for on our firmly resisting their unjust attempts can we alone depend on these attempts ceasing to be made." †

In 1823:—

" The frequent recurrence of our present difficulties must be expected until some change takes place in the footing upon which our intercourse with the Chinese is carried on. The contempt of foreigners, engendered and fostered by the abusive terms in which they are spoken of by the officers of Government, the want of police regulations, and the defenceless state in which we are placed, by the difficulty of access to the magistrates, leaves us exposed to assaults of all descriptions: and if self-defence is not received as a plea in cases of homicide, no in-

---

* Second Appendix, p. 524.
† Second Appendix.

dividual can, for one instant, be considered safe."*

On the 18th November, 1828 :—

" After a mature deliberation upon the griev-ances, which we have detailed in the preceding paragraph, we came to a determination, that it was incumbent upon us to meet them by a strong remonstrance, calculated to put a stop to further aggression : experience having proved, that no-thing can be expected to be obtained from the Chinese by concession; which only becomes an inducement to attempt further invasion of privileges."†

On the 23d October, 1830 :—

" The Chinese authorities have doubtless been encouraged in their demands by the two instances of successful intimidation above re-lated : and were the slightest disposition of concession evinced by us at the present moment, it cannot be doubted that they would be em-boldened to proceed to fresh acts of aggression."

—" We therefore came to the determination that firm and deliberate resistance to the line of conduct followed by the government, afforded the only hope of avoiding a series of indignities and insults, as well as of establishing the security of person so essential to the conduct of the trade."‡

---

* Auber, p. 297.

† Second Appendix, &c. p. 576.

‡ Second Appendix, &c. p. 442.

On the 15th December, in the same year:—

"We cannot avoid remarking, that the proceedings of last year appear to have made a considerable impression; and it must be admitted, as repeatedly demonstrated in the history of our intercourse with this country, that a firm opposition to the encroachments of the government generally, produces a favourable inclination towards us, after the subjects in dispute are terminated."*

In 1831 :—

"The existence of a powerful and influential body in your representatives in this country, has opposed the only check to the evils and embarrassments to which foreign commerce is continually exposed. *We believe that no effectual remedy will be found for them, until it suit the purposes or policy of Great Britain to assume, in its turn, the attitude of dictation, which would readily demonstrate the weakness of this Government.*"†

Truly, indeed, did the Select Committee observe, in their despatch of the 28th January, 1830:—"That the more important, the more valuable are the interests at stake, the more do they require the protection of firmness, on which our hopes of their security for the future

---

* Second Appendix, p. 444—5.
† Auber, p. 336.

can alone be placed with confidence!"* Alas! however, to what little purpose were all these representations and remonstrances addressed to the Committee at Leadenhall Street!

Such, then, are the two principal sources from which have long flowed the serious inconveniencies and wrongs which the British traders to China have now to encounter; and at this peculiar conjuncture, at so great a disadvantage, unless their just expectations from the Government of their country, be realized. They seek nothing unreasonable, nothing inconsistent with the welfare and honour of their country, nothing unjust towards China, or calculated to disturb the peaceful relations between that country and Great Britain. Who, indeed, can have a deeper stake in the contrary line of policy, than those whose interests, "whose fortunes, and livelihoods," as they themselves express it, are entirely dependent upon the preservation of our commercial intercourse with China?

There can, or at least ought to be, but one wish in this country, and that is, to cultivate the China trade, on fair and honourable terms. The only difference of opinion that can arise, is as to the *mode* of doing so. One class of persons is found asserting that the proper, the only mode of doing so, is to buy tea of the Chinese on any terms they choose to dictate, however degrading,

* Second Appendix, &c. p. 580.

however absurd, however unreasonable, however oppressive,—and be thankful! on the following grounds : That the Chinese are a great, power-ful, and peculiar people, with whom it is purely optional to continue or refuse permission for us to continue our intercourse, since they are not, nor ever were, or will be, bound by any *treaty ;* that, in the absence of any treaty, the law of nations prohibits any attempt to enforce our supposed claims upon the Chinese ; and that, even were it otherwise, the Chinese having never, as it were, entered into the society of nations, rightly refuse to recognize the law of nations; that their peculiar character is such as to render any attempt at coercive measures both inhuman and abortive ; and that, in short, rather than abate an iota of their pretensions and usages, in consequence of a threatening demonstration of foreign force, the Emperor of China, to adopt the wild and chimerical sug-gestion of Mr. Auber, "following the alleged example of one of his predecessors, when the cultivation of cotton became the occasion of dis-turbances in his kingdom, *of ordering the plant to be destroyed, might deal in the same manner with tea !"**

---

* Auber, p. 402.—"The growth of tea is chiefly confined to hilly tracts not suited to the growth of corn."—*M'Culloch.*

And yet a writer pretending to acquaintance with the sub-ject, has gravely stated his apprehension lest the Chinese should be induced, by our refractoriness, *to convert their tea plantations into rice fields !*

It is believed that the foregoing paragraph contains a faithful statement of the general principles upon which the policy of the East India Company was based,—of the views now entertained by those whose interests are identical with those of the late Company, and who are actuated by feelings of hostility towards those now prosecuting the trade upon the new system. It is the object of the ensuing pages to demonstrate shortly the fallacy of all such reasonings,—to appeal, in doing so, from the ignorant and prejudiced, to the liberal and intelligent portion of the community; and guard them against the artful misrepresentations propagated by bigotry and self-interest.

"As regards China," observes Mr. Auber, "we resort to a country in which we have not a foot of ground, and where we are confined to one port, at which our permanent residence is doubtful. . . . . The habits, manners, and customs are quite foreign to our own. Their laws are also frequently violated by those who are [appointed to be] their administrators and guardians; where their treatment of foreigners is proverbially contemptuous; and in their commercial dealings they have no scruple at imposition, if circumstances favour the practice. Such is the people with whom we seek to maintain an intercourse. . . . . China has rejected every effort made by us, as well as by almost

every other European state, to form a commercial intercourse with her, upon those principles
which govern commercial relations with other
countries."*

So speaks the late Secretary of the East
India Company; and his observations are in-
contestibly correct, except the last, which is
only partially so. It may be readily admitted,
as an abstract proposition, that however unreasonable and faithless they may be, no attempt
could be justifiable to gain by force a settlement in their territory. It has become, however, a matter very important to ascertain, how
far the Chinese are bound, by their conduct
during a long series of years, while in the course
of reaping the benefits of a commercial intercourse, which they themselves have uniformly
sanctioned by acquiescence, and even *invited*,
as will be presently shewn, by professions of
good will, and readiness to carry on trade with
us, *on the faith of which* we have been induced
to enter into vast speculations, to construct a
system of commercial dealings on a very expen-
sive and permanent scale, for the supply to this
country of an article of indispensable use to our
population, and an almost indispensable source of
revenue to our Government; involving the fortunes, and even livelihoods, of hundreds of thou-

---

* Auber, pp. 38-9.

sands of persons, the subjects of a great and independent nation : whether from all this is not to
be implied a tacit agreement on the part of the
Chinese, to carry on trade with us on equitable.
principles; such an one, in short, as, if broken,
will warrant us in compelling an observance of
good faith; of that " *customary* law which,
from motives of convenience, has by tacit but
implied agreement, prevailed, not generally indeed, among all nations, nor with so paramount
utility as to become a portion of universal voluntary law; but enough to have acquired *a prescrip-
tive obligation* amongst certain states, so situated
as to be mutually benefited by it."*

But, it is said, the Emperor of China has an
unquestionable right to permit or refuse us intercourse with his dominions ; to impose such
conditions as he may think fit; and that where no
treaty exists, nothing prevents him from, at any
time he pleases, withdrawing, restraining, or
modifying such permission.† Such observations
as these are, it is conceived, quite beside the
real question now in dispute : which is, not
what were the original rights of China, as an
independent nation, — what she might have
done, or refused to do, in the first instance;
but, what are the rights of China, *now;* whether
her own acts have not restricted and limited
those rights, and imposed upon her certain obli-

---

* Vattel, Prelim. note 7.   † Auber, pp. 39. 394-5.

D

gations, and subjected her to certain liabilities, from which the principles of justice,—of the law of nations,—forbid her to retreat.

Were it necessary to resort to abstract reasoning upon the subject, the following short paragraph, from a distinguished writer, (Vattel) might be referred to, as containing a striking statement of the principles regulating mutual commerce between nations. " All men ought to find on earth the things they stand in need of. In the primitive state of communion, they took them wherever they happened to meet with them, if another had not before appropriated them to his own use. The introduction of dominion and property could not deprive men of so essential a right; and consequently, it cannot take place without leaving them, in general, some mean of procuring what is useful or necessary to them. *This mean is commerce;* by it every man may still supply his wants.— Things being now become property, there is no obtaining them without the owner's consent; nor are they usually to be had for nothing; but they may be bought or exchanged for other things of equal value. *Men are, therefore, under an obligation to carry on that commerce with each other, if they wish not to depart from the views of nature. And this obligation extends also to whole nations, or states.* It is seldom that nature is seen to produce in one place, all that is neces-

sary for the use of man.   One country abounds
in corn, another in pastures and cattle, a third
in timber and metals, &c.   If all these countries
trade together, as is agreeable to human nature,
no one of them could be without such things as
are useful and necessary; and the views of
nature, our common mother, will be fulfilled.
Further,—one country is fitter for some kinds
of product than another; as, for instance, fitter
for the vine than for tillage.   If trade and barter
take place, every nation, on the certainty of
procuring what it wants, will employ its land
and its industry in the most advantageous
manner, and mankind in general prove gainers
by it.   Such are the foundations of the general
obligation incumbent on nations, reciprocally to
cultivate commerce."*

Without discussing the question, whether
the Chinese are absolutely warranted, in justice
to their fellow-nations, in shutting out all the
rest of the world from any participation in the
benefits of so prodigious a portion of the most
desirable parts of the earth,—even when that
participation would be attended with corresponding advantages to themselves,—it may be
contended that China *has long since surrendered
such rights*, and is no longer in a position to
enforce them, as against the British nation;

---

* Vattel, Book II. Chap. ii. Sect. 21.

that her conduct, during the last century or two, has amounted, not merely to a simple per-mission to us to carry on our trade with her, but has conferred upon us *perfect* rights, such as are accompanied by the right of *compelling* the fulfilment of the corresponding obligations. "But," it may be objected, in the language of Vattel, "a simple permission to carry on com-merce with a nation, gives no perfect right to that commerce; for, if I *merely and simply permit* you to do any thing, I do not give you any right to do it afterwards in spite of me.— You may make use of my condescension as long as it lasts; but nothing prevents me from changing my will."* This proposition of Vattel's, guarded even as it is in its terms, must be taken, subject to considerable limita-tions. If nation A, by a long course of conduct in commercial intercourse, from which she has derived great advantages, leads nation B to form the reasonable presumption that she will continue such intercourse on equitable terms, on the strength of which, nation B goes to great expense, and incurs a heavy risk in constructing a permanent commercial establishment,—surely nation A can never be at liberty, in such a case as *this*, which can never be called a case of "*mere simple permission*," arbitrarily to "*change her will!*"

---

* Vattel, Book I. Chap. 8. Sect. 94.

It is a reasonable and salutary rule of our municipal law, that a party shall always be bound by his admissions, when they have been such as have *induced a third party to alter his conduct ;** and that as strong an admission may be implied from mere silence and acquiescence, whilst certain acts relating to the observing party's rights are being done, as could be founded on the most explicit declarations and acknowledgments.† These are maxims founded on common sense, on justice, on the fitness of things; and, as the observance of them, therefore, between man and man, is inculcated by our municipal law, so there is no reason whatever why they should not be equally beneficially

---

* Hearne v. Rogers, 9 B. & C. 577.

† See the cases of Jarratt v. Leonard, 2 Maule & Selwyn's Rep. 265. Morris v. Burdett, 1 Campbell's Rep. 218 ; and Starkie's Evidence, vol. ii. 37.—Thus, the member of a trade, the constant course of which is to give credit, cannot turn round upon his customer, and say, " I insist upon being paid in ready money." Our courts, in such a case, would answer, that the customer has a right to assume that he was dealing upon the usual terms. Again, according to the ordinary rule of English law, the member of a firm may, if he please, dissolve the partnership immediately, by his secession : but if long leases have been taken, and heavy expenses incurred for the accommodation of the firm, this rule is changed,—and the law then presumes that there was a binding though tacit agreement that the partnership should continue as long as the period specified for the continuance of the lease.—See *Smith's Mercantile Law*, p. 9.

applicable to nation and nation, which, as all jurists admit, are "*moral persons*, possessing an understanding and a will peculiar to themselves, and being susceptible of obligations."*   Let us, now, apply these principles to the case of Great Britain and China.

From whatever motives, the Viceroy of Canton, so early as the year 1678, " INVITED the English to settle a factory there ;"† and in 1806, we find the Emperor of China thus writing to his "reverently submissive tributary" the King of Great Britain :—"Your Majesty's Kingdom is at a remote distance beyond the seas, but is observant of its duties, and obedient to its laws; beholding from afar the glory of our Empire, and respectfully admiring the perfection of our Government.....   With regard to those of your Majesty's subjects who, for a long course of years, have been in the habit of trading to our Empire, we must observe to you, that our celestial Government regards all persons and nations with eyes of charity and benevolence, and always treats and considers *your* subjects with the utmost indulgence and affection.   On their account, therefore, there can be no place or occasion for the exertions of your Majesty's Government."‡ —There are many

---

* Vattel, Prelim. Sect. 1.
† Milburn, vol. ii. p. 408, 1st ed.
‡ Auber, 217-8.

indications of a similar disposition on the part
of the Emperor of China towards the British
traders, to be found in the history of our intercourse; but it is not necessary to cite them.
It is sufficient for the argument, that from
motives of convenience and advantage to his
people, the Emperor has permitted us to trade
with them for nearly a couple of centuries ; and,
jointly with ourselves, has organized a very
extensive, costly, and effective machinery for
carrying it on.   Millions on millions have been
thereby interchanged between the two nations ;
British capital, to an immense extent, has been
embarked in the traffic ; we are content to
carry it on at a very great disadvantage,—compelled, for instance, as we are, to travel ten
thousand miles thither and back again, and to
incur all the risks of so many and such
perilous voyages.   Having done all this, with
the knowledge and consent of the Chinese
Government, we now deny their right abruptly
and arbitrarily,—either directly and with violence, to expel us from China ; or, equally
effectually to attain that object, by imposing
ruinous exactions, and inflicting such insults
and degradations as would render it impossible
for us, with a due regard either to individual
or national honour, to continue our intercourse.

It is a sound and settled principle of law,
applicable equally to nations and individuals,

that no one shall be permitted to do that *indirectly*, which it would be unlawful to do *directly*. Should, therefore, China attempt to pursue this latter course, she would sin against justice.* Is it excusable, on any principles of common equity, that the Chinese should be at liberty to continue our trade upon the precarious footing upon which it has long stood, and still stands;—that our ships, laden with most valuable cargoes, after a six months' voyage, should be suddenly prohibited from entering the Canton river; and, when on the point of return, freighted with tea, after having paid all the enormous and dishonest duties exacted from them, should be forbidden to leave it, at the mere caprice of the local authorities, on grounds the most ridiculous and wicked?—A trumpery affray between a drunken Chinese and a foreign sailor; a thoughtless violation of some petty and often vexatious Chinese custom; a dispute between the Viceroy and some Hong Merchant, as to the amount of duties claimed;—*and the whole trade is stopped:* —" whole fleets detained when on the point of sailing!"† " In the situation in which trade is placed, it is liable to be interrupted at the ca-

---

* See a striking suggestion contained in the Narrative of Mr. Chapman. Appendix to Lords' Rep. p. 264.

† Auber, p. 296.

price of one individual; and, should the Viceroy for the time being chance to be rather more ignorant, and, at the same time, more violent in disposition, than his predecessor, a complete interruption to the trade must inevitably ensue."*

Surely, conduct such as this amounts to a gross violation of the implied contract between the two nations;—one based, as we have seen, "on a tacit consent or convention of the nations that observe it towards each other."† The authorities on national law agree that, in analogy to the regulations of municipal law, there must be a reasonable notification in point of time, of the intention not to be bound by this customary law.‡ "Any state, *on giving notice* that she chooses no longer to abide by a particular custom, may set it aside, *provided the time* that she selects for this notification be not where a case may have arisen, or be contemplated, upon which the custom would operate."‖

Unless, therefore, we are to discard all principles of right reasoning and sound construction of the rights and liabilities existing between

---

* Second App., &c. p. 505.

† See authorities cited in the case of Benest v. Pipon; Knapp's Rep., 67, and Martin's Law of Nations, 356. Fennings v. Lord Grenville, 1 Taunt. 248.

‡ Id. Ibid.

‖ See 1 Chit. Commerc. Law, p. 29.

nations, we have abundant evidence to show that China has contracted—has imposed upon herself—the obligation of continuing to us a permission to trade with her, on fair and reasonable terms. " But," it is said, " *there is no treaty*— and in the absence of a treaty, there cannot exist any such obligation as that spoken of." It is true that there is no formal treaty solemnly and in so many words agreed upon between the two nations; that the Emperor chooses now to reject all attempts to procure one. Surely, however, we are warranted in contending, that in analogy to another regulation of our municipal law,— one of obvious reasonableness and utility,—*e.g.* a right of way over the ground of another, which after a certain number of years' use, confers by prescription, an indefeasible right to the enjoyment of that right of way, and is supported by the supposition of an original deed of grant of that easement;—the trade which the Emperors of China have suffered to be carried on for nearly a couple of centuries, may be reasonably presumed to have had its origin in a treaty— even of the most explicit and formal description. Let it be borne in mind again and again, that the advantages of this trade are not all on one side, but reciprocal—and have been acknowledged to be so, by China. It is mere trifling to talk of her being now at liberty to disregard the law of nations, on the ground of her having never deigned to recognize it. She has been long too far committed by her conduct towards this country. We have already seen that in 1678 she *invited* us to settle a factory at Canton ; the Emperor has himself personally—and repeatedly through his Viceroy—sanctioned our intercourse, and even laid down the terms on which it might be carried on. In 1715 the supercargoes stipulated for eight articles or conditions, according to which the trade might be carried on with China, and which were deliberately and solemnly conceded.* Passing over many other instances, we find, at length, a complete recognition of our trade, in the Chinese Government's requisition to this country, in consequence of the meditated abolition of the East India Company's charter,—calling upon us to send out forthwith to China " a chief," [*i. e.* a Superintendent,] whom the Canton authorities might recognize and deal with as such —and who, as we shall shortly see, was accordingly sent. And in the face of all this we are told that we are without any remedy, however injured or insulted by the Chinese—" for that they are in no wise bound to continue their intercourse one moment beyond what pleases them !" Is it not an outrage on common sense

---

* Nearly all of which, however,—as far as they were beneficial to us,—have been since abrogated.

and common honesty to hold that they ought to be at liberty thus to play *fast and loose* with us? They have an adequate " consideration," to adopt an English law-term, for entering into the contract, in the revenue they derive, and will derive at all times hereafter, from our trade— and their obligation is therefore complete. Let them occasionally indulge in what rhodomontade they will, in affected disdain of the benefits of trade, experience abundantly proves that they are as sensible of them as we are,—and, if need be, even prepared to make considerable sacrifices to secure its continuance. The compulsory removal of our trade would be followed almost immediately by infinite disorder in China: for is it likely that the people would quietly submit to the loss of so fruitful a source of employment and subsistence? " We beg to draw the attention of your Honourable Committee," say the Select Committee (24th Sept. 1814), " to the anxiety shewn to recal Sir George Staunton, as affording a proof that however the Chinese Government may declare in their edicts that no benefit arises to the Chinese Empire from the foreign trade, and that it is permitted only from pure benevolence; yet when endangered from their unjust proceedings, properly and firmly resisted, it will be found that they are most fully aware of the reciprocal advantages of commerce, and most anxious for its preservation."* To say nothing, however, of prudential considerations on the part of the Emperor of China,—it must be conceded that he lies under a moral and political obligation to continue to us a commercial intercourse with his people, on equitable principles. Whoever grants to another a particular privilege, is considered also as conferring, by implication, all the means necessary for the complete enjoyment of it: and if it is clear that the Emperor of China is under an obligation to suffer our trade to continue, he is also bound to secure to us the means necessary for carrying it on with safety —subject, of course, to those laws and customs of the Empire which are not glaringly inconsistent with honour and good faith. But how stands the fact? We have already seen the President of the Select Committee complaining to the Court of Directors, in 1815, of the fearful extent to which the properties, liberties, and even lives of foreigners were in the power of the local authorities at Canton,—the arbitrary and reckless manner in which they exercise their irresponsible authorities; and similar language might be adopted in characterizing the conduct of the Chinese from that period up to the present. The trade is bowed down with the most grievous and increasing exactions; personal

* Second Appendix, &c. p. 527.

liberty is constantly restricted within narrower limits.* Accusations—as we have seen—of the most disgusting and dreadful description are publicly preferred against our innocent countrymen, in formal proclamations and edicts, with the view of making them hateful to the lower orders of the Chinese.

" It is almost impossible," says Mr. Holman, " to convey to the reader an accurate idea of the insulting nature of these edicts, by any means short of printing them in full ; but the indecencies to which they bear reference, and the gross language in which they are clothed, would render such a course reprehensible. In one of these proclamations they charge the British merchants with the worst description of levity and vice—and found upon this pretence, an excuse for depriving them of the use of native servants, whom they strictly forbid the local authorities to permit them to hire."†

---

* Occasionally the gentlemen land on the opposite side of the river for the pleasure of a walk ; but in such cases they run the risk of being insulted and even assaulted by the natives, who follow them with coarse invectives, and often carry their hostility so far as to throw stones at them. Whenever they leave their boats, they seldom escape injury, and even on the river, in passing, the rude and audacious natives will sometimes fling stones and missiles at the foreigners.—Holman, vol. iv. p. 74.

† Voyages and Travels, vol. iv. pp. 107-8.

" The Chinese *assault* either the ships, or their boats"—say the Select Committee, in 1823—"and when they meet with a return, demand large sums of money for *wounds!*—by working on our timidity to offend the recent imperial edict on the subject of the liability of foreigners to suffer death, even though the hazard of their own lives requires their defence. The success which their extortions have occasionally met with, invites the return of new assaults. That all ranks of Chinese are sensible of our situation in this respect, is too clearly evinced by the perpetrating of such dangerous impositions by many in a very low class of life; and the reward that success in their demands sometimes affords, is a sufficient inducement to attempt it, without any consideration as to the result—occasioning consequences the most prejudicial to the commerce, and even the lives of foreigners."*

Again, in the same year, we find the Select Committee continuing their complaints:—

" Thus we see our situation, clearly made responsible for the acts of between two and three thousand individuals who are daily coming in contact with the lowest of the Chinese, and exposed to assaults so wanton, and often so barbarous, as well as to robberies so extensive, that

---

* Second Appendix, &c. p. 567.

self-defence imposes upon them the necessity of
attacking their assailants in a manner from
which death must often ensue. A great and important commerce is instantly suspended—
whole fleets, at times detained—ourselves liable
to seizure—and to be the medium of surrender-
ing a man to death whose crime is only self-
defence, or obedience to orders, or else to lend
ourselves to the most detestable falsehoods, in
order to support a fabricated statement which
may save the credit of the officers of the China
Government. Can the Honourable Company
wish their servants and their trade to remain in
this degraded—this dangerous situation?"* It
would be an easy matter, alas! to swell the cata-
logue of such grievances. They meet the eye
of the inquirer at every page of the documents
relating to Anglo-Chinese affairs; and are calculated to make one's heart swell at once with
astonishment at the supineness of the British
Government, and with indignation at the audacious and unprincipled conduct of the Chinese.
At the moment that generous and flattering
speeches concerning foreigners are flowing from
the royal lips, at Pekin, those unoffending and
too-confiding foreigners are subjected to the
most systematic oppression at Canton! Their
persons and properties are placed in perpetual

---

* Auber, 293-4.

jeopardy; their characters are defamed, in terms
insufferable even to be thought of; a series of
petty personal provocations and annoyances is
kept up unceasingly; the laws of nature are out-
raged—for their wives are separated from their
husbands,* and compelled to reside eighty miles
off—at Macao—an insult perfectly gratuitous;
the laws of China are forbidden to be appealed
to; the regulations of trade are so contrived as
to secure the most grievous *and increasing* impositions; the whole trade is stopped in the most
capricious and injurious manner; and, under all
these circumstances, how can a British merchant continue to carry on his commercial pursuits at Canton, but at the sacrifice of his personal safety and self-respect? Where is there
to be found any law, either of nature or nations,
justifying such a state of things as this? There
is, as Lord Mansfield used to say, *no magic in
words*—and we must recollect that the " law of
nations" is but " the just and rational application of the law of NATURE to the affairs and
conduct of nations"†—and that it is a fundamental maxim of that " *natural* law, that it is
the duty of nations to fulfil their engagements,

---

* In this respect British merchants in China are worse off
than were even our West Indian slaves, who were protected by
act of parliament from such a refinement in persecution as the
compulsory separation of wives from their husbands.

† Vattel, Preface– *prope initium.*

E

whether express *or tacit.*"* China is a large
and fortunate branch of the great family of mankind,—but she is not therefore exempt from the
obligations of that law which God himself has
prescribed for the conduct of his creatures. Is
the avalanche less subject to the law of gravita-
tion, than the minute particles that may happen
to be detached in its descent? In vain shall
China attempt, much longer, to insist upon
such selfish and unnatural pretensions and immunities; there are those upon the earth who
will not tolerate her arrogance, or wickedness;
who will rise and resent those injuries which
WE have meanly submitted to for centuries.†

Is, then, the trade of China to be continued,
and on terms consistent with the honour of the
British nation? If the voice of Great Britain
answer this question in the affirmative, a very
different tone and style of policy must be forthwith assumed, from that which has hitherto so
unfortunately been adopted. Great as are the

---

* Vattel, Preface, p. xvi.

† The Chinese have, on various occasions, fully recognised the obligations of the law of nations. The ambassadors of Shah Rokh Mirza had brought as a present to the
Emperor, a noble horse, which, unfortunately, threw the Emperor in hunting. That great and just personage ordered
the ambassadors to be loaded with chains. Their death
even was apprehended, but the Emperor pardoned them,
yielding to the entreaties of his ministers, who represented
to him the disgrace of violating the law of nations, in the
person of an ambassador.—See Auber, p. 72.

sacrifices we have made to secure this valuable trade, long as we have carried it on, important as are the relations and responsibilities it has entailed upon us, we should forfeit for ever our character in the society of nations, whose eyes are upon our movements in this matter,—were we, on light grounds, now to succumb to the Chinese,—to be bullied and terrified by their absurd swagger and airs of intimidation, into a surrender of our just and hard-earned rights and privileges. At the present moment these considerations press upon us with uncommon force. Having seen fit recently to alter altogether our system of commercial intercourse with China,— a measure which must be presumed to have been thoroughly and wisely considered before it was adopted,—we shall become the laughing-stock of the world, if the direct effect of our elaborate legislation be, either to shut us out altogether from China, or place our intercourse upon an infinitely more precarious, oppressive, and ignominious footing than ever,— as will infallibly be the result, if we be not now fully alive to the nature of our claims upon China, and prepared to assert them with resolution and vigour. Is there any one who doubts the justice of these observations? Let him meditate upon a recent illustration of their truth,—the melancholy and most humiliating reception and fate of Lord Napier! The death of that nobleman,—the insult offered, through his person, to the King of Great Britain,—IS YET UNAVENGED! Not a syllable of remonstrance or of threat has it yet called forth from the British Government! Surely this outrageous transaction cannot be duly known or appreciated in this country.

Lord Napier was sent out to China at the express instance of the Chinese Government.*

In 1831, the Viceroy of Canton stated, in an edict, issued with reference to the change which he understood as likely to take place in the mode of carrying on the British trade :—

" I hereby issue an order to the Hong Merchants, that they forthwith enjoin my command on the said nation's Chief, early to send a letter home, that if, indeed, after the thirteenth year of Taou Kwang, the Company be dissolved, it will, as heretofore, be incumbent to deliberate and appoint a chief who understands the business, *to come to Canton,* for the general management of the commercial dealings; by which means affairs may be prevented from going to confusion, and benefits remain to commerce."†

His Lordship was ordered by our Government

---

* The Order in Council (9th December, 1833,) referring to this circumstance, stated, "that it was expedient that effect should be given to such *reasonable* demands of the Chinese Government." This is as it should be. Would that it might be considered as an intimation that henceforth this country would acquiesce only in the " *reasonable*" demands of the Chinese !

Auber, p. 335.

to reside within the limits of the port of Canton
and not elsewhere.   On his arrival at Canton,
the Viceroy refused to receive his letter, announcing his mission, unless it were sent through
the Hong Merchants,—a step which Lord
Napier, for sufficient reasons, declined to adopt.
His right to proceed to Canton, without an express permit, was disputed, though European
boats had for years past been permitted to do so,
without any necessity for such a document.
After three or four weeks' negotiation on this
point, all British trade was stopped from the
16th August till the 27th of September, to the
grievous injury of the British merchants having
valuable cargoes then in port, and waiting at the
mouth of the Canton river, till permitted to enter
the port.   During this period, the Chinese went
the length of interdicting all supply of provisions
to Lord Napier, and cut off his communication
with the ships of war.   His health, under these
harassing circumstances, began to suffer to
such a degree, that it became necessary to remove him from Canton,—the only means of
effecting which, was in a Chinese boat, provided
by the Government, who wantonly detained the
dying Nobleman five days on the passage from
Canton to Macao, ordinarily accomplished in
two days, subjecting him, at the same time, to
other indignities and cruelties ; under the combined effects of which he sunk, and expired

shortly afterwards at Macao. Such was the
audacious treatment experienced at the hands
of the Chinese, of the representative of the King
of Great Britain,—despatched at the express
instance of the Chinese! Such the insults
offered to the British nation, and submitted to
in meekness and silence!* Such is an indica-
tion of the spirit which animates the Chinese
towards the British traders, at the present important conjuncture,—such the degraded and
insecure position occupied by the latter! What
insult or injury is there which the Chinese may
not, after this, consider themselves capable of
inflicting upon the British trader, with impunity? What must be their opinion of the spirit
of Great Britain, indeed so " reverently submissive," to conduct so audacious as this? Dropping, however, for a moment, all considerations
as to the decency—the policy of such submis-

---

* " It may afford an useful illustration of the insolence of
the Chinese authorities, and their impudent bravado," says
Mr. Holman, " to add, that an edict was issued by the Emperor, when he received the Report of the Governor, (in
which all the circumstances relating to the affair of Lord
Napier were detailed in a most distorted manner, and in a
style at once false and exaggerated), ordering that part of
the honours which the Governor and his officers had been
deprived of for their previous neglect, should now be restored
to them, for the course they had taken; but particularly for
' having driven the barbarian eye (Lord Napier) and others
out of the port!' "—*Holman's Voy.* vol. iv. p. 176.

sion and acquiescence with reference to the
national *honour*, let us inquire *what will be its
direct effect upon the position and interests of
the trade*. It is impossible to foresee to what
lengths of outrage and oppression the Canton
authorities may be emboldened to proceed,
should their unwarrantable treatment of His
Majesty's representative be permitted to pass
without even a show of remonstrance : the consequence of which, it is but too probable, would
soon be developed in such a systematic aggravation of existing evils, as would lead to constant collisions and stoppage of trade. When
these interruptions occurred during the East
India Company's monopoly, their united influence and capital enabled them sometimes to
make a stand against the Chinese, and to sus-
tain the heavy commercial losses attendant on
the struggle. Widely different, however, would
be the case under present circumstances; when
the free traders, pursuing each his separate and
disunited view, and having no common head
recognized by the Chinese, must fall a sacrifice,
in detail, to their well-combined machinations.
There is, indeed, a painful probability of these
apprehensions being realized, unless the British
Government bestir itself betimes in the matter.
If the Chinese seize upon the present moment,—-
the present critical position of our commercial
relations,—to inflict any injury upon our traders

that avarice and insolence combined can dictate, surely it is, correspondingly, the duty of
our Government, at the same trying moment, to
make a firm and decisive demonstration in
favour of our oppressed fellow-subjects at
Canton.   Surely it should be the pride, as it is
certainly the interest and duty, of a wise Government to preserve, as well as to extend the commercial advantages which may have been acquired by the energy and enterprise of its people.
" The prince," says the illustrious commentator
upon the laws of England, " is always under a
constant tie to protect his natural-born subjects
at all times and in all places;"* more especially
when they are engaged in so vast a national
enterprise as that of the China trade, and that
in the manner and on the system specially
appointed by their Government.   A heedless,
timorous, or temporizing policy *now* adopted
towards such a people as the Chinese, who have
recently evinced such symptoms of contempt
and injustice towards us, would not only be
attended with the most destructive consequences
to the trade, but reflect intense dishonour upon
the   national   character, — inviting   additional
aggression.   Even the peaceful, pliant and con-
ciliatory Directors of the East India Company
ventured more than once to hint their right to

---

* 1 Blackst. Comm. Book I. c. 10, p. 370.

resent the injurious conduct of the Chinese.
"If the Chinese Government," said the Court
of Directors in 1816, "were, in an unfriendly
inhospitable spirit, by *inequitable conduct* to
force to a close a pacific intercourse which has
subsisted so long, *and in which this country has
embarked so great a capital,* it could hardly fail
to resent such a harsh and injurious proceeding."* Two years afterwards, we find them
roused for a moment from their lethargy by
some fresh recital of grievances, and intimating,
" *that they were not in any degree inclined to surrender or abandon the immunities and privileges
hitherto enjoyed by our factory,* AND TO WHICH
THE IMPERIAL EDICTS HAVE RECOGNIZED
OUR JUST CLAIMS!"†

Why then should not the British Government appear promptly and decisively in support of such interests as are at stake, even, *if
necessary,* to a degree of sternness, in the assertion of our rights against such lawless invasion?
" Because,"— say the East India Company,
and those who adopt their mode of thinking,—
" it may throw the Emperor into a sublime
sulk, and that would lead to our sudden and
final exclusion from their commerce." This
answer, before alluded to, first of all admits
most unwarrantably that we have not hitherto

---

* Auber, p. 257.   † Ibid. 280.

acquired any rights against the Chinese, which is directly at variance with the above-cited declarations of the Directors themselves in their despatches in 1816 and 1818;—secondly, that so do we value the tea-trade that we are willing to carry it on under all possible disadvantageous and dishonourable terms; or, lastly, that having a valid right, on the principles of moral and international law, we have not the power or spirit to assert that right. The first and second of these fallacies have already, it is hoped, been disposed of. If we are, as a nation, afraid to look boldly and steadily at the real position we occupy, or have a right to occupy—in truth, the less worthy are we of retaining possession of its advantages. If we will absurdly and pusillanimously go out of our way to hunt after subtle and far-fetched pleas for abandoning or restricting our rights, disregarding the great and universal pinciples of national law, which really support those rights, —we had better at once act up to our principles, and commence our descent from the position we at present occupy in the scale of nations !

Granting that we have just and substantial rights to vindicate against the Chinese,—that these rights are so important as that the assertion of them becomes a matter of capital importance to us in a national point of view,—that we have the means to assert those rights, and the inclination to adopt those means,—what is the obstacle? Are the Chinese so formidable in a warlike point of view, so determined of purpose, united in action, and skilful in council, as to render it inexpedient to adopt the necessary measures, however desirable?

Every one whose opinion is worth consulting, who has had due opportunity for observation, and gives his evidence in an unbiassed manner, assures us that the Chinese, however disposed to adopt a magnificent style of language, are much more apt to waste the idle artillery of words in official interdiction, than to resort to serious and really threatening measures in assertion of their rights. It is indeed, with them, invariably—a flourish of trumpets, and enter Tom Thumb! Listen to the marvellous language adopted by the Viceroy (27th October, 1830), in addressing our Committee.

" The celestial Empire benevolently nourishes, righteously rectifies, and gloriously magnifies a vast forbearance. How is it possible that for driblets of men in a petty—petty barbarian factory,‡ *troops* should be moved to exterminate!!! [*sic.*]" But the said Chief, and others, could not explain this intention (in the

---

* " It is impossible," says the Translator, " by the word *foreign* (le) to give the spirit of this sentence."

Hong Merchants' threat); they stupidly listen
to the teaching of traitorous persons, and forthwith presumed, in opposition to inhibitions, to
order guns and arms to be brought up, and
arrayed them at the door of their factory.
This is still more wild and erroneous. Only
try to think—if indeed the said foreigners had
among them an illegality of a very important
nature — I, the Governor, would instantly fly
to report to the Emperor, *and the Government
troops would gather together like clouds, exterminate them, and leave a perfect vacuum!!!* How
could their guns and arms they have brought,
presume to oppose such a force?"* Is this the
sort of fulmination at which Britain must turn
pale?

The Chinese will at one moment adopt language pregnant with direful import, and, at the
next, if encountered by even a show of serious
resistance, sink into the most ignominious submission, and resort to ridiculous subterfuges, in
order to escape from the consequences of their
own folly and audacity.† "I have always
entertained but one opinion," says that shrewd
and candid observer, Mr. Holman, "in reference
to our connexion with, and policy towards
China. We have treated them with too much
forbearance; they have all the braggart, as well
as all the recreant qualities of cowardice in

---

* Second Appendix, &c. p. 422.　　† Ibid. p. 457.

their nature. If we were to make a decided demonstration of hostility, we should speedily obtain all that we require at their hands. A few British men-of-war would shatter the flimsy armaments of China with as much facility as our presence, even in slight numbers, and without power, keeps their vagabond multitudes in check, in the suburbs of Canton."* And again —" They are uniformly overbearing and insulting to all those who happen to be in their power, but cringing and abject to those who exhibit a determination to resist them."†

The Emperor of China has, in truth, neither the inclination nor the power to resort to hostile measures, in order to destroy our trade, or banish us from his territories, *if he saw us disposed to offer a serious resistance.* He is far too sensible- of our importance—of his weakness, and our strength,—even in spite of the artful and iniquitous means adopted by the local authorities to keep him in the dark as to the real state of his relations with this country, by forbidding, intercepting, and falsifying all our attempted communications. It is to further such mischievous purposes as these that they forbid our acquisition of their language, and deny us access to the higher and supreme authorities. The

---

* Holman, Voy. & Tr. vol. iv. p. 109.   † Id. ib. 68.

wide-spread corruption* and utter imbecility existing in his empire,†—the general poverty of his
people,—are too painfully apparent to the Court
at Pekin to admit of its sanctioning a breach, and
resort to extreme measures, with so powerful a
nation as the British. It is as much as they
can do to conceal "the rottenness in the state
of Denmark" behind a glaring grandiloquence.
A glimpse of one or two of our men-of-war
stationed off the north-eastern coast of China,

---

* " The Chinese, impenetrable to every thing else, are
never impenetrable to bribery. They are the most corrupt
people on the face of the earth. I really believe that China
might be purchased out and out, if a largess sufficiently
great could be procured."—*Holman*, vol. iv. p. 63.

† The following circumstance related by Mr. Holman, will
illustrate the truth of this observation. Every one knows the
great exertions of the Chinese Government to prevent the importation of opium: see the power they have to carry their
decisions into effect! " Friday, October 15th, 1830.—Some
friends of mine, who were returning from Whampoa to-day,
saw a very amusing fight upon the river between two mandarins' boats and a smuggler. One of the former fired a gun
at the latter, which was immediately returned, although he
was making off; and as he pulled fifty oars, assisted by his
sails, he soon distanced his pursuers. Meeting, however,
three boats of his own calling, he joined them, and *they all
drew up in line to give regular battle to the mandarins!*
The plan of the smugglers was a little curious. It being flood
tide, they formed their line across the river, above the mandarins' boats ; they then brought their carriage guns to their

would send a thrill of consternation through the whole empire, and do more to incline the Chinese to listen to the dictates of reason and justice than centuries of "temporizing" and submission to insult and oppression. Experience ought by this time to have shewn us that it is a foolish and useless policy to attempt to gain the confidence of the Chinese by exhibiting, as was constantly enjoined by the East India Company, a servile deference to their innumerable and absurd peculiarities and customs. An ob-

---

sterns, wetted their boarding nettings, to prevent them from catching fire, (which were all ready to trace up), and, presenting their sterns, they pulled in that position towards the mandarins' boats, which, however, were glad enough to make a precipitate retreat. Thus, *in open day, only a few miles below Canton, four smugglers resisted with impunity the Government of the country !*"— And all this, too, after " an edict of the Emperor had been published, ordering the local authorities to exercise all their power to prevent the growth and importation of the poppy."—" Tremble," said the poor Emperor, " and obey !"— *Holman*, vol. iv. p. 89—92.

It would be easy to multiply such instances of the wretched imbecility of the Chinese Government. One more must suffice. " Notwithstanding there is a rigid prohibition against Chinese books being sold to foreigners, Professor Newmann found no difficulty in procuring all that he desired to obtain ; and to prevent their being seized on their way to the ship, he paid a stipulated sum, for each case, *to the mandarin*, who betrayed the trust to his government so openly, that he actually *sent some of his men to pack them at the Professor's lodgings !*"— Id. ib. p. 46, (n).

servance of very many, if not most of them, is inconsistent with the free spirit—the sense of what is due to self-respect—of the enlightened nations of Europe. Hateful, indeed, is—or ought to be—the idea of smothering or compromising such feelings, from considerations of mere traffic and gain.* " The free and high-

---

* The following is a very remarkable instance at once of Chinese folly and wickedness; and affords a lively specimen of the character of the people whose manners and requisitions the East India Company required their representatives in all things to respect and observe :—" Some time ago an affray occurred at Kum-sing Moon, in which a foreigner was deliberately murdered by three or four natives, who overpowered him in the affray ; and to conceal the murder, instead of burying the body, they cut it to pieces, carried it in a fishing boat out to the roads, and cast it into the sea. This statement was obtained from their own confession ; no remnant of the man was ever found. On the other side, a native was wounded in the posteriors with small shot, the parts mortified, and he died within twenty or thirty days. The local government caught the natives who wounded the foreigner, and they demanded that the foreigner who fired the shot, which wounded and caused the death of the native, should be found and delivered up to them. With this demand it was not practicable to comply. Week after week they reiterated the order to have the " *foreign murderer*," as they called him, delivered up. At last, despairing of compliance, Government has connived at a Hong Merchant, a leader among that responsible body, having, for 400 or 500 dollars, bribed some ignorant half-foreigner, about Macao, to personate the foreign murderer, and have put this confession into his mouth, in order that his life may be safe, and he be banished from China, after

minded nations of Europe," says the calm and
philosophic Malte Brun, " will never admit the
arrangements of a tyrannical police, the annoyance of a childish etiquette, and the ' great
walls,' which have been erected for interrupting
the communications of the human mind."* The

---

the farce of trial and report to the Emperor shall be gone
through. This is the purport of the confession which the
Chinese admire for its ingenuity. —' The foreigner who was
killed at Kum-sing Moon, was my elder brother. When I
saw the natives murdering him, I ran up, and stood forward to
rescue him, at which moment a fowling-piece, I had fastened
to my back, went off, and shot the native, who has since died.
We two brothers were the only children of an old mother, who
has now no one to take care of her. I beg for mercy, that I
may return home and wait on my mother in her old age.'

" These circumstances were intended to be kept secret from
foreigners, but common fame and some tell-tale divulged them.
The foreigners protested to the Governor of Canton against an
innocent man being thus implicated, although by his own
ignorance and folly. The Governor has over and over again
denied the man's innocence, but says the man has delivered
himself up, in which there is some merit, and has confessed the
facts, which will save his life, inasmuch as the deed was purely
accidental, quite unintentional, — therefore he will not be
required to forfeit his life. All this the governor, the judge,
the Kwang-chow-foo, and other mandarins concerned, as well
as the foreign and native public, know is perfectly untrue ; but
with this fiction of law they are proceeding, and have reported
to Peking in substance as above, and are now waiting, with the
man in confinement, for the Emperor's answer. The man was
subsequently liberated unhurt."—*Holman*, vol. iv. p. 164—6.

* Malte Brun, vol. ii. p. 607.

time for attending to such trifles has passed away, as have occupied so much of the anxious attention of the East India Company and its local representatives.   Is it not revolting to common sense and common humanity, to think that the mere appearance of an English lady at Canton—that lady the wife of Mr. Baynes, our first resident merchant,—that an English in-valid's venturing to use a *sedan*, the common conveyance among the respectable Chinese,— has each of them led to the most alarming and protracted misunderstandings — to insulting " Orders " and " Edicts "— to threats of sus-pending the whole British trade—to negotia-tions and correspondence of a long and most harassing description ?   Yet such have been the facts !*   It is repeated that graver consi-derations must henceforth occupy the attention of those who carry on the trade with China, and a sterner spirit be exhibited in enforcing the claims of reason and justice.   If we should un-fortunately find the Chinese turn a deaf ear to all our remonstrances, and bent upon continuing in full force the galling system of imposition and insult from which they have so long reaped so rich a harvest; if, above all, they should pre-sume to inflict upon us so vast an injury as the

---

* See Auber, *passim*, and Second Appendix, Paper A, pp. 407—8, 446.

interdiction of our trade (which is of all things the most improbable): then will have arrived the time when our Sovereign would be *bound*— bound by the duty he owes his subjects, and authorized by the law of nations—to interfere on their behalf, and protect them from such grievous injuries. This he might do, in the first instance, by issuing letters of marque and reprisal, "which are grantable by the law of nations whenever the subjects of one state are oppressed and injured by those of another, and justice is denied by that state to which the oppressor belongs."*

The Emperor of China, by ratifying the acts of the local authorities in their outrageous treatment of Lord Napier, has rendered himself responsible for such treatment; it has "become a public concern, and the injured party is to consider *the nation* as the real author of the injury, of which the citizen was only the instrument."† Surely we should be able to show, before proceeding to such extremities, that we have "ineffectually demanded justice, or that we have every reason to believe that it would be in vain for us to demand it."‡ "Justice is refused,"

---

* 1 Bla. Com. bk. i. c. 7. p. 258.

† Vattel, Book ii. c. 6. § 74.

‡ Vattel, Book ii. c. 18. § 343; Grotius, De J. Belli ac Pace, Book ii. c. 2. §§ 4-5.

says Vattel, " in several ways: first, by a denial of justice, properly so called—or *by a refusal to hear your complaints or those of your subjects, or to admit them to establish their rights
before the ordinary tribunals.*"* If this latter be,
in the opinion of an enlightened writer on international law, of itself a sufficient cause for the
granting of letters of marque and reprisals,—
what abundant cause exists for resorting to the
same measures, in the accumulated wrongs
which the Chinese have already heaped, and
still threaten to heap, upon the subjects of
Great Britain ! If China chooses to follow up
the insult she has offered to us in the person of
Lord Napier, by abruptly excluding us from
her trade—by breaking the agreement which
her own conduct, as well as ours, shows to have
been in existence for more than a century,
surely we may adopt the language of *the Court
of Directors,* in 1816, and say, that " we could
hardly fail to resent so harsh and injurious a
proceeding."† A ship of the line, together with
a couple of frigates and three or four sloops,
would suffice—we are told,‡ " to put a stop to
the greater part of the external and internal
commerce of the Chinese Empire—to intercept

---

* Vattel, Book ii. c. 18. § 350.

† Ante, p. 19.

‡ See " Petition of the British subjects at Canton to the
King in Council."

its revenues in their progress to the capital, and
take possession of all the armed vessels of the
country." There is another way, says Mr.
Holman, of bringing the Chinese to their
senses.

" If Great Britain were to take possession of
Macao, garrison it with native troops from
Bengal, and declare it a free port, it would be
one of the most flourishing places in the East."
In this opinion, however, this intelligent tra-
veller has been misinformed, for Macao would
be worse than useless to Great Britain, owing
to the humiliating tenure on which it is held
from the Chinese, and its want of a suitable anchorage for any but vessels of the smaller class.
If any island is taken possession of, it should be
in a central part of China,—CHUSAN for instance, as suggested by Sir James Urmston,
formerly chief of the Company's factory. Then
indeed might we hope to see it become one of
the most flourishing places in the East; " for,"
continues Mr. Holman, " the Chinese are so
fond of smuggling, that they would not hesitate to trade with foreigners if they could be
assured of receiving protection; and there is
no doubt that they would use all those arts
of bribery with their own countrymen, which
would be necessary to promote their own
ends, and which are so irresistible to the
equivocal integrity of the Chinese. By these

means, therefore, there is not a doubt that a very extensive and productive trade might be established with China, and very important advantages secured to the British nation. When these facts are so self-evident," well may the writer add, " it is wonderful that some measures have not been taken to secure the commerce and to protect the merchants from the insults and obstacles which are now so much complained of, as well as to lower the bullying and imperative tone which the Chinese at present think fit to adopt in all their mercantile transactions."*

The British merchants trading at Canton desire, however, neither to contemplate nor to suggest a resort to such extreme measures, unless forced upon us by the failure of more peaceful means. Their inclinations, as well as their interests, incline them to be men of peace. They are satisfied that their interests—that is, the interests of the nation—may be effectually secured without it, and that our commercial intercourse with China may be easily, speedily, and peaceably placed upon an honourable and secure footing. Great Britain need show herself to the Chinese, not in a threatening, but simply a resolute attitude, in order to secure that grand *desideratum*,—a direct access to the

---

* Holman, vol. iv. p. 50.

court at Pekin; where such cogent representations might be made to the Emperor,—such a demonstration of the weak and embarrassed state of his kingdom, of the solid and permanent advantages he may reap by conceding our few and reasonable demands, and the serious consequences of persisting in an obstinate and insolent disregard of them, as would, in all human probability, lead to the happiest results. Could the Emperor but be made to see that his brother monarch of Great Britain—the King of a great and independent nation —was perfectly in earnest about the matter,—that at length he was tired of the tyranny and injustice to which his subjects at Canton have been so long subject, and resolved upon obtaining satisfaction for the deep insult offered to him through his representative Lord Napier;—the whole history of China shows that the Emperor would not be long in deciding which of the alternatives to adopt, or finding a suitable and stately pretext for making the requisite concessions. We desire him to drop for ever the arrogant and offensive language so long adopted by himself and his ministers, in speaking of the King of Great Britain and his subjects; to give reparation for the fatal insults offered to Lord Napier, and to the national honour, in firing at her flag,—as well as remuneration for the losses we sustained by the detention of our ships during the stoppage of our

trade on that occasion ; to extend to our fellow-
subjects at Canton the full protection of the
Chinese laws ; to forbid the longer infliction by
the local authorities of the intolerable indignities and impositions under which our traders
have so long suffered, and to accede to commercial arrangements that may be reasonable
and mutually beneficial.   This is the short sum
of all that it is desired our Government should
demand from that of China.   The honour and
interests of the country equally require it.   It
is ignorant trifling to talk of " treating the ro-
domontade and verbiage of the Chinese with
the contempt it deserves."   It cannot be denied
that, as stated by the Canton merchants, in
their " Petition" to the King in Council, " the
disabilities and restrictions under which our
commerce now labours, may be traced to a long
acquiescence in the arrogant assumption of supremacy over the people and monarchs of other
countries, claimed by the Emperor of China for
himself and his subjects ;"—and that "they are
forced to conclude, that no essentially beneficial
result can be expected to arise out of negotiations in which such pretensions are not decidedly repelled." . . . " That they most seriously apprehend that *the least concession or
waiving of this point*, under present circumstances, could not fail to leave us as much as

ever subject to a repetition of the injuries of
which we have now to complain." It might
have been deemed politic, in our early intercourse with the Chinese, to acquiesce in their as-
sumptions—to pass over their vain-glorious and
bombastic phraseology, or treat it as an amusing
absurdity. We had then to gain a footing
where we had not a tittle of claim even to be
tolerated on or near their shores; where we
were strictly "tenants by sufferance,"—and besides, could not have contemplated the effects
such acquiescence would have produced prac-
tically upon their treatment of us. Now, however, circumstances are indeed changed. We
have learned by the severe experience of two
centuries, the truth of the representations above
made; and may depend upon it, that so long as
the Chinese find us tolerate their styling our
King " a reverently submissive tributary" and
his subjects " profligate barbarians,"—they will
treat us accordingly. Hence the *absolute necessity* of demanding the discontinuance of such
language—even supposing it to be consistent
with the *dignity and honour* of Great Britain to
submit to the degradation of carrying on trade
upon such terms.

So far back as the year 1815, we find the
President of the Select Committee at Canton—
Mr. Elphinstone,—thus indicating, to the Court

of Directors, the most advisable course then to pursue, in order to remedy evils of which we have now even far greater cause to complain:—

"There appears to me no mode so likely to prevent these injurious consequences (*i. e.* " an entire stoppage of the trade with China,") as that of establishing a direct and frequent communication between the two governments. Missions on a far more moderate scale than the former embassy may prove fully as efficacious. No *particular act or appearance of favour or concession* need be expected from the Chinese Government. The beneficial effects will be, in placing the British nation on a more respectable footing with respect to China; and their frequent communications, independent of the superior advantage an embassy will now possess—of English interpreters—will prove to the provincial authorities, that remonstrances can be conveyed to Pekin."* Following up this suggestion, and profiting by subsequent experience—carefully considering, moreover, the very peculiar position of affairs at the present conjuncture, it is submitted that his Majesty's Government would act wisely in adopting the suggestions of the present Canton merchants: who, after " lamenting that such authority to negotiate, and force to protect from insult, as the

---

* Second Appendix, &c. pp. 503-4.

occasion demanded, were not entrusted to his
Majesty's Commissioners," — and expressing
their " confidence, without a shadow of doubt,
that had the requisite power, properly sustained by an armed force, been possessed by
Lord Napier" they would not now have " to
deplore the degraded and insecure position in
which they are placed, in consequence of the
representative of our Sovereign having been
compelled to retire from Canton, without having authority to offer any remonstrance to the
Supreme Government, or to make a demonstration of a resolution to obtain reparation at
once for the insults heaped upon him by the
local authorities,"—humbly pray—

" That his Majesty would be pleased to
grant powers plenipotentiary to such person of
suitable rank, discretion, and diplomatic experience, as his Majesty in his wisdom might
think fit and proper to be entrusted with such
authority : and that he should be directed to
proceed to a convenient station on the Eastern
coast of China, as near to the capital of the
country as might be found most expedient, in
one of his Majesty's ships of the line, attended
by a sufficient maritime force, which—they are
of opinion—need not consist of more than two
frigates, and three or four armed vessels of light
draft, together with a steam vessel, all fully
manned ;"—and that he might be thus placed in

a position to demand the reparations and concessions above suggested. Scarcely any additional expense—if *that* could be an object in
such an affair as this—need be incurred by this
country, in adopting this course of policy; since
the costly establishment which, in consequence
of their exclusion from Canton, we are now
maintaining (with hardly any functions to exercise) at Macao,—may be greatly reduced;
and our Indian squadron, already in commission, might be directed to cruize as a fleet of
observation along the coasts of China, instead
of lying at some of the Indian ports, which are
usually found very unhealthy to their crews.
If the occasion should not be deemed to require
in the first instance, the services of a special
plenipotentiary, the Admiral might be charged
with a letter from our Government, to the Emperor, referring to the manner in which Lord
Napier was received and treated, as a reason
for desiring a communication with his Imperial
Majesty, with a view to come to an understanding on this painful subject, as well as on
the grievances from which the trade is suffering.*

Any attempt to renew negotiations at Canton

The harbour of Amoy, in Fokien, from its depth of
water, facility of access, and sheltered position, is admirably
adapted to afford a secure anchorage for his Majesty's ships,
even of the largest size.

should be avoided ; since, besides involving the probable consequence of a suspension of the trade—as happened in the case of Lord Napier —it would be sure to prove useless, from the circumstance of the local officers of that province not being authorised by their own government to treat with foreign powers : *while they are, at the same time, the parties against whose wrong- doing it is especially wished to appeal.* The esta- blishment of the Hong Merchants is one of the most artful and successful engines of oppression and extortion that was ever devised. They are the only medium through which foreigners can carry on trade with the Chinese empire; and have a very obvious motive for making mischief when they have the opportunity, between their superiors and the foreign traders; *i. e.*, their jealousy of foreign merchants, and fears least they should become too powerful and wealthy, and at length supersede themselves. " The Hong Merchants," say the Select Committee, (1st January, 1831,) " have, unhappily, ever been jealous of the concession of any privileges which add to the respectability of foreign re- sidents. They proceed also upon the principle, that the greater the depressed state of foreigners, the less likely is their own responsibility to be in- volved."* The tremendous liabilities of the Hong

---

* Second Appendix, &c. p. 445.

Merchants, also render it, in a manner, absolutely necessary for them to inflict incessant impositions upon the foreign traders. As an instance of this it may be stated, that the whole expense of the immense preparations recently made by the local government to oppose the expected advance towards Canton of his Majesty's frigates, after they had passed the Bogne, has been extorted from the Hong Merchants; and as but a few of them are really solvent, the only means of meeting such a demand is—*combining to tax both the import and the export trade!*

If, finally, his Majesty should see fit to adopt the above suggestions, there remains one observation—already alluded to—to be most respectfully pressed upon the attention of ministers;—that our plenipotentiary should be clothed with sufficient powers to enforce, if necessary, the assertion of our rights. It is an acknowledged maxim in all negotiations, that the surest preventive of war is an unequivocal manifestation of our being neither unable nor unprepared, on its becoming necessary, to resort to it. The moment our negotiator lets it be perceived that he is precluded by his instructions from adopting such a course, whether to protect the rights of our merchants, or vindicate the respect due to his official character, he may be assured that all his arguments will prove unavailing and can tend only to betray his weakness; while, it is

equally certain that the acute policy of the
Chinese will, at the very outset, be invariably
exerted to make him develope under what instructions he is acting; what are the limits to
his sufferance, and what the extent of his
powers to retaliate in case of insult or injury.
This they will soon bring to light, *by such a
studied system of privation and disrespect, as shall
compel him to show his strength, if he have any, or
wanting* this, to flounder through a course of
alternate opposition and unavoidable submission, which cannot do otherwise than end in his
defeat.

Such, then, is the present state of our commercial relations with China. Such are the
principal sources of our present grievances; such
our prospects and opportunities; such, in short,
the claims of the British Merchants at Canton ;
such the duties of the British Government. The
time has arrived when a decisive step must be
taken. We must, at once, make up our minds
either to abandon for ever our dear-bought
commercial intercourse with China, or take
effectual measures for securing its continuance,
and that upon a safe, advantageous, honourable,
and permanent footing. We must resolve upon
vindicating our insulted honour as a nation, and
protecting the injured interests of our commerce
—or, in the face of Europe,—with " all appli-
ances and means to boot"—fully sensible of the

magnitude of the interests at stake, as well as
the ease with which they may be protected and
perpetuated—humble ourselves, nevertheless,
in ignominious submission, at the feet of the
most insolent, the most ungrateful, the most
pusillanimous people upon earth.

OUTLINE

OF SOME

LEADING OCCURRENCES IN THE

HISTORY OF THE CHINA TRADE.

[The few following details will serve, it is hoped, at once to
illustrate and fortify the more important statements and
conclusions contained in the foregoing pages.]

THE records of our early intercourse with the
East clearly establish one most important
fact, that the difficulties experienced in opening
a trade with China were the result rather of the
jealousy of rival Europeans, than of any decided
aversion to foreigners on the part of the natives.*

---

* The following " Abstract from Chinese statistical papers,
respecting European intercourse with China," is illustrative of
Chinese ideas respecting foreign trade.

" When foreigners of the Western Ocean, who were called
Franks, came, and, like others, talked of conveying tribute to
court, they abruptly entered the district of Ting-quan, and
with tremendous roar of their guns, struck terror into all, both
far and near. A *yu-she* wrote to court, and procured a prohibition of all foreign ships."

Subsequently to this prohibition of foreign trade, the Fooyuen Sen-foo addressed his Majesty as follows :--

G

In support of this assertion, it may be instructive to take a brief glance at some of the leading occurrences.

"A great part of the necessary expense, both in the officers of government and people, is, at Canton, supplied by the customs levied on merchants. If foreign ships do not come, both public and private concerns are thrown into much embarrassment and distress. It is requested that the Franks may be permitted to trade.

"Three or four advantages result from permitting the Franks to trade: first, in the beginning of the dynasty, besides the regular tribute of the several foreign states, a small per-centage was taken from the remainder, which was adequate to the supply of the government expenditure. This is the first advantage. Second, the treasury appropriated for the annual supply of the army of Canton and Kwang-sy, is entirely drained; and our dependence is on the trade to supply the army, and to provide against unforeseen exigencies. This is the second advantage. Third, heretofore Kwang-sy has looked to Canton for supplies. If any small demand is made on that province, it is unable to comply with it. When foreign ships have free intercourse, then high and low are all mutually supplied. This is the third advantage. Fourth, the people live by commerce. A man holding a small quantity of goods sells them, and procures what he himself requires. Thus things pass from hand to hand, and in their course supply men with food and raiment. This is the fourth advantage. The government is therefore assisted—the people enriched— and both have means afforded them on which they may depend.

"At a former period (1520) the foreign mart was removed to Tien-pih, about one hundred miles from Canton. In another year (1534) Kwang-king, an officer of that district,

The Portuguese enjoyed nearly a century's priority of intercourse with the celestial empire, (from A. D. 1517); and, free from the competition of any other European nation, traded at various ports, subject only to occasional contentions, the result of acts of violence and injustice characteristic of those times,—perpetrated, perhaps, on both sides. In 1555, they appear to have concentrated themselves at Macao, where they built a town. We hear of their ships frequenting the port of Canton in 1578, and trading along the coast of China; but in 1631, in consequence of some disputes which had arisen with the natives, they were restricted to their own settlement at Macao.

Such was the state of affairs when, in 1634, the Portuguese, in consequence of the capture of their own vessels by the Dutch, were induced to charter an English ship, the London, from the Company's factory at Surat, for a voyage from Goa to Macao; and a convention

---

having received a bribe, wrote to the superior officers of government, requesting to remove the mart to Macao, on condition of an annual duty of 20,000 pieces of money. Thus the Franks, in an under-hand way obtained admission into the country. They then began and built lofty houses. The merchants of Foo-kien and Canton flocked to them. They, in time, received addition to their numbers, and all the small surrounding nations, who formerly came thither, were afraid, and shunned them. Hence they assumed a sole right to the place."

was made, that the English should have liberty of trade at all the Portuguese settlements in Asia.

On the faith of this agreement, Captain Weddell, with three vessels under his orders, was despatched from London about the year 1635, by a company having the title of " Courteen's Association," (in which Charles the First was a shareholder), for the purpose of making the first attempt, on the part of the English, to establish a trade with China. He carried with him, by way of credential, a letter from King Charles I. to the Portuguese Governor of Macao, who, however, in direct violation of the convention, peremptorily refused admittance to the British vessels. Nor did the opposition of the Governor stop here, for, as Captain Weddell found, on applying to the Chinese for permission to "traffic freely with them, on the same footing as our European precursors," the treacherous Portuguese had sent emissaries to Canton for the purpose of exciting a prejudice against the English.*   In this object, by the

---

* It is remarkable that some twenty years before this period a strong prejudice against the English prevailed in China, by reason of the piracies committed by the Dutch, under the British flag, on the Chinese coasting junks. " But the Company's agent at Japan exposed this deception, by making the real facts known in China, and the good report of Englishmen (the Company's records state) was in consequence higher

double operation of bribes and aspersions on our
national character, he so completely succeeded,
that the courteous disposition manifested by the
natives towards Captain Weddell in the first
instance, gave place to feelings of so hostile a
nature, that the Chinese commenced making
warlike preparations, and actually fired several
shots at his barge, when going on shore for
water.

Incensed at this unprovoked outrage, "the
English fleet (consisting of three small merchant vessels and a pinnace) displayed their red
ensigns, and took a position before the castle,
whence the Chinese discharged many balls at
them before they could bring a piece of ordnance to bear, to return the fire., After fighting
two hours, perceiving the courage of the Chinese to fail, Captain Weddell landed about a
hundred men, at sight of whom the Chinese, in
great confusion, abandoned the fort, the English
entering, planting on the walls the British flag,
and carrying on board all the ordnance found
in it."

The result of Captain Weddell's exploit was
his obtaining a patent for free trade, with liberty
to fortify on any place out of the river. This
invaluable privilege was, however, rendered

there than ever." See *Lords' Report on Foreign Trade*,
1821, p. 284.

nugatory by the East India Company's hostility to "Courteen's Association,"* which was in consequence suppressed.

In 1644, the Chinese empire was conquered by the reigning Tartar dynasty. The southern provinces, however, were not reduced to submission for many years, during which the greatest anarchy prevailed ; the coasts being scoured by native junks, which, acknowledging no law, plundered all who were not strong enough to protect themselves. In order to cut off the resources of these marauders, the Tartar government resorted to the extraordinary expedient of compelling the inhabitants of the southern shores to retire thirty Chinese miles towards the interior, and renounce all intercourse with the sea. The Portuguese, by especial indulgence, were excused from removing into the interior, but were prohibited from navigating their ships, or engaging in foreign trade. Entire stagnation of commerce was the

---

* " Courteen's Association " was established by King Charles I., to participate, with the East India Company, in the India trade, because (as the preamble to their license states) " the East India Company had neglected to establish fortified factories or seats of trade to which the king's subjects could resort with safety ; had consulted their own interest only, without any regard to the king's revenue, and, in general, had broken the condition on which their charter and exclusive privileges had been granted to them."

result, and Macao was reduced to the greatest distress.

On the return of a more settled state of affairs, the Tartar government became desirous of a revival of foreign trade, and, accordingly, in 1678, the Viceroy of Canton *invited the English to establish a factory at that place.* Unfortunately, however, the English company, influenced by an apprehension of offending the Chinese chieftain, Koxinga, or rather his successor, with whom they had dealings at Amoy and Formosa, (then held by him in defiance of the Tartar Government) did not avail themselves of this desirable overture, which is the more to be regretted, as Koxinga's power was shortly afterwards extinguished. On this occurring, the English turned their attention to Canton, but found themselves forestalled by their ancient rivals the Portuguese, who, in 1682, by a bribe of 24,000 taels (about 8000*l.* sterling) per annum—obtained from the Governor of Canton an edict prohibiting the merchants of that place from "trading with strangers."* Accordingly, some English vessels which visited the coast about that period, were " warned off" by " a message from the General of the Tartar fleet, announcing that the Portuguese had petitioned him to turn

---

* See East India Company's Records, laid before the House of Lords in 1821.

out all strangers," and " that there was a mutual obligation between the Emperor and the Portuguese not to permit a trade with any other European nation."

In 1685, the Emperor KANG HE issued his famous edict by which the ports of the empire were declared to be open to all nations. It does not, however, appear that any change of policy at Canton was produced by this edict, which, therefore, it is probable that the governor of that province, influenced by the annual bribe of 8000*l.* from the Portuguese, contrived to evade.*

---

* That the impediments to foreign trade in China arose rather from the rivalry of Europeans than from any disinclination to commerce on the part of the natives, is further exemplified in the fact, that there are no records of the English trading with Formosa during the thirty-eight years of its occupation by the Dutch (from 1624 to 1662); while the Chinese chieftain Koxinga, who dispossessed the Dutch, invited foreigners to trade; and accordingly, during his rule, in 1670, an English factory was established. Koxinga's successor was conquered by the Tartars in 1681.

In like manner, when the Dutch attempted to open a trade with China, they were opposed not only by the Portuguese at Canton, but by the Jesuit missionaries at Pekin, who prejudiced the Emperor's mind by informing him " that they were only possessed of a small part of a country, which they forced by rebellion, from their lawful sovereign; and thereupon became pirates at sea, robbing all they met with in order to support their power on land."

The first notice, in the East India Company's published records, of an English vessel visiting Canton, is found in a communication to the Directors from the Factors at Surat, who state that a ship of 500 tons had traded at the former place in 1694; subject, however, to many vexations and extortions. There appear to be no details of our intercourse for the twenty years immediately subsequent to that period; but it is stated by Mr. Auber, the Secretary to the East India Company, that in 1715, " the intercourse with Canton had assumed somewhat of [the character of] a regular trade."

The Hoppo, or superintendent of foreign trade, invariably admitted our supercargoes to an audience, at which they stipulated, through their Linguist, for the observance of a series of articles, generally to the following import :—

1. *Free trade with all Chinese without distinction.*
2. Liberty to hire Chinese servants, and to dismiss them at pleasure. English servants committing any offence to be punished by the supercargoes, and not by the Chinese.
3. Liberty to purchase provisions, &c. for their factory and ships.
4. No duties to be chargeable on the reshipment of unsold goods, nor on stores, such as wine, beer, &c. expended in the factory.
5. Liberty to erect a tent on shore for repairing casks, sails, &c.

6. English boats, with colours flying, to pass and repass the Custom houses without examination, and the sailors' pockets not to be searched.

7. Escrutoires and chests to be landed and reshipped without examination.

8. The Hoppo to protect the English from all insults and impositions of the common people, and the mandarins.

Not only, however, (as before stated,) have these reasonable privileges, with the exception of one or two of the least important, been abrogated by the Chinese, but disabilities and restraints the most humiliating have been inflicted on the European traders.

The wily Chinese were not slow in perceiving the value of a trade which allured so many Europeans to their shores, excited so eager a rivalry among them, and furnished the resources of those costly bribes which they had been accustomed to receive from the Portuguese. It therefore became their study to secure a continuance of the rich harvest, and seeing Europeans so lavish of their money, as the price of restraints upon commercial rivals, they naturally enough viewed a system of restrictions and disabilities as the readiest engine for extracting those gains which had gradually ceased to flow in, from the voluntary impulse of the mutual rivalry cherished by their foreign visitors.

Thus it became, to use the words of Sir George Staunton, " a part of the system of Chinese policy with respect to all foreigners, to restrict and restrain them *to the utmost to which they will submit;* but not to drive them to despair, and thus destroy a trade of considerable importance to the Chinese empire, and absolutely essential to the prosperity of one of its provinces."*

All offices, from the highest to the lowest, under the Chinese Government, being objects of sale, the holders consider themselves justified in resorting to every possible extortion in order to obtain the largest return for the capital expended on the purchase ; and the distance of Canton from the capital, enables the authorities

---

* The importance attached by the Chinese to foreign trade is exhibited in a Memorial to the Emperor from the Governor Fooyuen, and Hoppo of Canton, dated March 1832 :—

" But this prosperous dynasty has shown tenderness and great benevolence to foreigners, and admitted them to a general market for a hundred and some scores of years, during which time they have traded quietly and peaceably together, without any trouble. *How then would it suddenly put a barrier before them, and suddenly cut off the trade? Besides, in Canton, there are several hundred thousands of poor unemployed people who have heretofore obtained their livelihood by trading in foreign merchandise. If in one day they should lose the means of gaining a livelihood, the evil consequences to the place would be great.*"

at the former place to indulge their rapacity to an extent never contemplated or sanctioned by the court of Pekin. In furtherance of their corrupt views, these provincial functionaries prohibit the Chinese from teaching Europeans the language, " on the ground that it might lead to their complaints reaching and troubling the Court." They thus removed all check on their malpractices; and being free to make any misrepresentations they pleased respecting Europeans to the Emperor, without. the smallest chance of being contradicted, they have been able by degrees to obtain his sanction to many parts of a system of oppression and abuse, the most ingeniously calculated for its object of extortion which it is possible to imagine.*

---

* " The Chinese officers of government are continually changing their duties from one province to another. The amount that may have satisfied the officer of one year will be found insufficient for his successor. Pleas and pretences for requiring donations under so despotic a government are easily found, nor are they readily evaded." [From a paper by Mr. Elphinstone laid before the House of Lords, 1821.]

" It is from a corrupt influence that the selection for the principal officers in the various local governments proceeds; the Mandarins in the enjoyment of the imperial favour at Pekin, disposing, in most cases, of the situations of profit and authority to those in the several classes of Chinese distinction who are enabled to give the best price. Hence it follows, as a matter of course, that in the appointment of a new Viceroy,

The Company's supercargoes appear, at first, to have resisted the impositions of the Chinese

---

or a new Hoppo, some irregular, illegal, or unauthorized practice is said to be discovered, for which penalties are threatened. These penalties are compromised by a bribe from those who are principally involved in the charge; and as it is the foreign trade which is best able to bear these exactions, it is to that source the Viceroys and Hoppos of Canton generally direct their first attention for the means of repaying the purchase money of their respective appointments, and also to enable them to accumulate as large a sum as possible during the few years (generally not more than four or five) they are permitted to hold those appointments. From the continued succession of functionaries, all owing their offices to the same influence, the venality of every branch of the service is perpetuated. So far as regards the foreign trade, this principle is the more detrimental, because from the shortness of the period to which the authority of each Viceroy and Hoppo extends, those officers have not sufficient opportunity to become completely acquainted with the whole detail of the foreign trade, whence they are of necessity obliged to place the more reliance upon the opinions and statements of the Hong merchants, and these, to serve their own purposes, generally impose upon their superiors such statements only as they think best calculated to answer the present emergency, whatever that may be; and, as some of the members of the Hong possess great wealth, the united accumulation of their predecessors and themselves in the same Hong, they have a corresponding influence with the local government, which is thereby induced to lend, at all times, a favourable ear to every representation they may make on points connected with the foreign trade of the empire." [From a paper which the Directors laid before the House of Lords in 1821.]

with becoming spirit. It was not unusual for
them to detain their vessels at the mouth of the
river until they had exacted an assurance of
proper treatment from the Canton authorities.
Failing to obtain such assurance, they had the
alternative of trading at Amoy; the threat of
doing which had, on more than one occasion,
the effect of bringing the Mandarins to reason.
It appears, also, that the supercargoes had sen-
tries to guard their factory; a wholesome pre-
caution which, like many others, has long since
been discontinued.

The Company's records, at a very early period,
furnish a striking illustration of the Chinese character. "A private British ship (the Ann), belonging to Madras had (in 1716) seized a junk belonging to Amoy, in satisfaction of some injuries
received at that port. The emperor, being informed of this, sent a special messenger to inquire
into the affair; and, on his report, ordered the
Mandarins, whose duty it was to see justice done
the Madras merchants, to be severely punished."

"1718-19, January 16.—The seizure of the
Amoy junk made the Chinese treat the English
better than formerly. The Emperor obliged the
Mandarins to make the owners satisfaction, and
confiscated the remainder of their estates.

"1719, July 29.—The trade in China last
year so good that Madras this year sent two
ships. The seizure of the Amoy junk had

caused the English to be better treated than ever."—*Lords' Report,* 1821, p. 279.

Yet, with this striking example before them of the Emperor's desire to do justice, and their long experience of the provincial authorities' proneness to do wrong, the East India Directors, in 1751, adopted the preposterous policy of " authorizing their supercargoes to expend such a sum as they might see fit in endeavouring to obtain for the trade relief from exactions !"*

Attempts to restrict the dealing of foreigners to a few licensed Chinese, in violation of the privileges granted in 1715, are frequently noticed in the early history of our intercourse, but they were generally counteracted by the decisive measure of detaining the ships outside the port until the restriction was removed.

In 1754-5, however, three years after the Directors authorised recourse to bribery, the following remarkable notice appears on the Company's records :—

" An attempt made [by the Factory] to get rid of the practice of the English finding security merchants; in consequence of which, merchants of credit would not trade with them, *and they were therefore on a worse footing* than other nations *who traded at the port.*"†

---

* Auber's China, p. 167. See this extraordinary fact commented upon, ante, p. 9.

† See Lords' Report, 1821, p. 293.

In 1759, two years after Canton had obtained a monopoly of the trade, when the authorities were no longer restrained by the apprehension that foreigners would resort elsewhere, the limitation of our dealings to a *few licensed* Chinese was made part of the established system of trade, and those individuals, designated Security or Hong Merchants, were regularly incorporated under the name of the " COHONG," with whom alone Europeans were permitted to deal; all transactions with other Chinese, excepting, indeed, petty shopkeepers, being declared illegal.

In 1771, the supercargoes congratulate themselves on having procured the dissolution of this obnoxious Cohong at the cost of 100,000 taels (from £30,000 to £35,000), which they actually expended on the occasion.* In 1779-80, however, the same Cohong appears again in full operation, and was made the instrument, as it has continued to be ever since, of levying an additional tax on foreign trade, under the designation of *Consoo Fund*, the origin of which is thus related. Debts amounting to 3,808,075 Spanish dollars, were owing by Chinese to British subjects, which the latter were unable to recover ; and on their representation of the fact to the Madras Government, Captain Panton, of his Majesty's ship Sea-horse, was requested

* See Auber, p. 178.

to proceed to China in order to urge payment, and having instructions from Admiral Sir Edward Vernon, and as well as from Sir Edward Hughes, to insist on an audience with the Viceroy. This audience, after some delay, and not without the use of threats on the part of the British commander, was obtained, when Captain Panton received a fair and satisfactory answer to his application.* Not so, however, was the

---

* " This measure had occasioned very serious alarms at Canton. The Chinese merchants who had incurred the debt contrary to the commercial laws of their own country, and denied, in part, the justice of the demand, were afraid that intelligence of this would be carried to Peking; and that the Emperor, who has the character of a just and rigid prince, might punish them with the loss of their fortunes, if not of their lives. On the other hand, the Select Committee, to whom the cause of the claimants was strongly recommended by the presidency of Madras, were extremely apprehensive, lest they should embroil themselves with the Chinese Government at Canton; and, by that means, bring, perhaps, irreparable mischief on the Company's affairs in China. For I was further informed that the Mandarins were always ready to take occasion, even on the slightest grounds, to put a stop to their trading; and that it was often with great difficulty, and never without certain expense, that they could get such restraints taken off. These impositions were daily increasing; and, indeed, I found it a prevailing opinion, in all the European factories, that they should soon be reduced either to quit the commerce of that country, or to bear the same indignities to which the Dutch are subjected in Japan."—*Captain King's Voyage in H.M.S. Discovery*, A. D. 1780.

result; the "satisfaction" ultimately granted being the payment of one-half only of the debts without interest, by equal instalments, extending over a period of ten years; this tardy payment being made, not from the pockets of the Chinese, but from the new impost on European trade, already alluded to, as the Consoo fund. This took place, however, after Captain Panton's departure.

In their evidence before the House of Lords,* the East India Directors avow it as their system, " to temporize with the insolencies and caprice of the Chinese Government ;" as " the servants of a commercial body, can bear many things which a King's officer could not, with due regard to the honour of his Sovereign, submit to." For this reason they opposed the appointment of a King's Consul at Canton, " as it might not become his office to submit to indignities which the servants of a body of merchants could endure without much disgrace."

Maxims such as these could not but be repugnant alike to the judgment and feelings of many of the Company's successive servants at Canton,† who, between a sense of duty, which

---

* See Evidence, Lords' Report, 1821, pp. 116 and 178.

† This is forcibly illustrated in a private letter (which has been published) from Sir Theophilus Metcalfe, chief of the

urged compliance with the instructions of their employers, on the one hand, and the dictates of

---

Factory, to the Chairman of the Court of Directors, respecting the proceedings of Sir Murray Maxwell, in battering the Bogue fort, and entering the river in 1816 :—

" Believe me, sir," he observes, " the acts of a Viceroy will ever continue arbitrary and unjust if not properly resisted. The trade only requires a check on his conduct and the extortions of other Mandarins at Canton, and I trust the cautious, judicious, and firm conduct of Captain Maxwell on this occasion will lay the foundation of placing the Company's trade on a steady footing, and receive that support from the ministers and court of Directors as will convince the Chinese that the blood of Lord Anson still flows in the veins of Englishmen. I might be told, *as President of the Factory, these are not the sentiments I should promulgate. In reply, I assert, they are the sentiments held in private by every man who has visited China in the last twenty years;* and it is only to be regretted that the continual victories gained by a few supercargoes should not have carried such conviction as to make these sentiments more agreeable. I am aware that they are not to be stated in a public letter; but as throughout life I have never disguised my opinions, I feel it my duty to convey them in some manner."

Again, Sir Theophilus adds, " If he (Captain Maxwell) conceived the ambassador wished, and his own judgment determined him to insist on entering the Bogue, I pointed out the fallacy of negotiation, and that *in China the act must be performed and then discussed.* Had any formal application been made it would have been refused, *not upon the laws of China, but the arbitrary pleasure of an hostile Viceroy;* and any proceedings contrary to his expressed will and pleasure would have proved very serious. If these ideas should be

their own better judgment and experience on the other, were betrayed into a vacillating and inconsistent line of policy. The utmost opposition, which, under such circumstances, they could offer to Chinese injustice, was generally feeble in its effect, and, when unsuccessful, as it often was, did more harm than good, inasmuch as it shewed the Chinese how easily their own passive perseverance could defeat it.

So sensible was Sir George Staunton of the impolicy of the Directors' views, that he attempts to qualify the nature of them by observing, "It will hardly be supposed it was intended here to recommend any disgraceful or humiliating compliances ; these, however flattering they may be for the moment to the vanity of the people with whom we have intercourse, can never permanently conciliate their good will; they will generally be found to invite oppression, and they invariably insure contempt. The practical consequences of such compliances in aggravating the evils they were designed to

---

held as too strong, I have only to request I may be judged by my public acts. Throughout my conduct in this present discussion, *I condemn myself for forbearance, at the same time I act from instructions,* and have only the alternative of endeavouring to convince the Court that absolute submission is not necessary !" &c. &c. &c.

(Signed)   " THEOPHILUS J. METCALFE."

remedy, the early history of the European intercourse with China has amply illustrated."

In 1784 occurred a tragical event, which
completed the degradation of the English character in the eyes of the Chinese, the supercargoes having, in order to obtain a renewal of
the trade, surrendered the innocent gunner of
the ship Lady Hughes, to be strangled by
the Chinese, in retaliation for the death of a
native, who was accidentally killed while the
ship was firing a salute. This occurrence the
supercargoes of 1823 remark, "inflicted indeli-
ble disgrace on all parties concerned."*

An anecdote from Cook's voyages,† however

---

* Auber, p. 295.

† Capt. King, during his continuance at Canton (1780)
"accompanied one of the English gentlemen on a visit to a
person of the first distinction in the place; the captain having
been previously instructed that the point of politeness con-
sisted in *remaining unseated as long as possible, readily submitted to this piece of etiquette;* after which he and his friend
were treated with tea, and some fresh and preserved fruits.
Their entertainer was very corpulent, had a dull heavy countenance, and displayed great gravity in his deportment. He
had learned to speak a little *broken English and Portuguese.*
After his two guests had taken their refreshment, he conducted them about his house and garden, and when he had
shown them all the improvements he was making they took
their leave." — *Cook's Voyages,* vol. iv. p. 243. Ed. 1793.
[Any one acquainted with China must, at once, perceive that
the person of distinction alluded to could not have been a
mandarin, but was a mere merchant.]

unimportant in itself, is given in a note, as strongly evincing the submissive spirit which then prevailed among the English in China.

Equally characteristic is the following extract from the Company's records :—

In 1781 Captain M'Lary of the Dadaloy, a private ship, learning, on his arrival at Whampoa, that war had broken out between the English and the Dutch, ventured on the unjustifiable proceeding of seizing on a ship with Dutch colours, as a lawful prize, and refused to resign her, when ordered to do so by the Chinese. " This led to a long and vexatious correspondence with the supercargoes, who were ordered to compel obedience, and threatened with fine and imprisonment. The matter was afterwards compromised by Captain M'Lary *dividing the booty with the Chinese, who then treated him with marked attention and favour, but continued to offer insults and injuries to the supercargoes, so great as to render it doubtful whether they would not be compelled to take to their ships.*" *

In early times the Chinese appear to have taken no cognizance of offences, committed by one foreigner against another, leaving them to the more equitable jurisdiction of the respective nations, whose subjects were implicated. An

---

* Company's Records, Lords' Report, 1821, p. 294.

affray, however, having taken place in 1754, between some English and French sailors, in which one of the former was killed, the Chinese, for the first time, exercised their jurisdiction in cases of this description, at the instigation (as the French allege) of the English; which, if true, is a very serious accusation, more particularly as the Chinese seized and executed an innocent Frenchman for the crime. The correspondence on the subject has been published. " It only now remains for us to know," say the French to the English, " the motive which could have induced you to demand justice *from the Chinese Government*, with so much importunity, for the man who has been killed. We can only think that you had no other intention than that of injuring our commerce ; but, gentlemen, in doing us a wrong, *you do it to posterity and to all the foreign nations that are here.*

" *It is morally certain that the Chinese will no sooner have taken cognizance of affairs between Europeans, than it will be no longer possible to preserve that liberty which all nations have hitherto enjoyed, and by their acting on this occasion, they would use it advantageously to search by force into our very privacies for persons charged with the slightest offence.*"—Since this occurrence, the Chinese have occasionally exercised their jurisdiction in such matters, and at other times have waived it, according to the caprice or convenience of the moment.

The East India Company's monopoly being now at an end, the foregoing details would not have been entered on, were it not of importance, and, indeed, quite indispensable, in the consideration of our future relations with China, to be fully aware of the circumstances which have preceded and originated our present unfortunate position in that empire. And the writer is much mistaken if it have not appeared that the disabilities under which we labour, are little more than must have been expected from the faulty system hitherto pursued.*

It has been usual to attribute Chinese restrictions on Europeans to the twofold impulses of arrogance and fear; but the writer thinks he has proved that avarice has operated with them as a more powerful motive than either; on the sound conclusion that their extortions could be best perpetuated by founding them on disabilities and degradation.

---

* It is with much regret the writer has come to this conclusion, which is at variance with the opinion he formerly entertained, before having instituted minute inquiries into the leading facts detailed in the foregoing pages.

SOME INSTANCES OF SUCCESSFUL NEGOTIA-
TION WITH THE CHINESE.

Allusion was made at page 13 to the spirited exertions of the East India Company's super-cargoes, on several occasions, by way both of remonstrance and resistance, when encountering Chinese oppression. It was also stated generally, that, notwithstanding all the embarrassments which fettered and restricted such operations, they were attended with a degree of success which affords conclusive evidence that only a moderate degree of firmness will suffice to procure the most important concessions from the Chinese. In justice to these supercargoes, and also for the information of those desirous of obtaining a clearer insight into the practical details of this question, the following instances have been selected.

The most remarkable was that which occurred in the year 1829, when the embarrassed state of trade, from increasing exactions, and the bankrupt condition of a majority of the ten or twelve Hong merchants, to whom foreign dealings are restricted, induced the supercargoes to suspend the Company's trade for several months. The result was a reduction, by Imperial sanction, of about 170*l*. in the port charges of every ship trading at Canton; while the exactions on the appointment of new Hong merchants, which had previously deterred applicants for the office, were ordered to be discontinued, and several accessions to their number accordingly took place,—thus relieving the trade from the paralyzing effects of a monopoly by two or three individuals. The compulsory separation of the sexes was discontinued, foreigners being permitted to enjoy the society of their wives and families at Canton, and other minor advantages were in course of acquisition.

Towards the end of 1830 some opposition was again attempted to the residence of foreign ladies at Canton. The Viceroy tried the effect of intimidation, and instructed the Hong merchants to threaten that Mrs. Baynes, the wife of the senior supercargo, would be seized and carried off, if she did not quietly quit Canton. The supercargoes on this, with great promptitude and resolution, ordered up 150 armed seamen, with two great guns, to protect their factory,—a guard which remained in Canton for about ten days, till the Hong merchants gave a written assurance that the ladies should not be molested,—the trade all this time going on with as much quiet and regularity as if there were nothing in dispute. Most unfortunately, orders arrived, a few days afterwards, from the Court of Directors, suspending from their situations, the spirited supercargoes, Messrs. Baynes,

Millett, and Bannerman, who had carried these reforms.   The Chinese took their cue accordingly: in the course of the season the ladies were obliged to quit Canton! Affairs indeed generally took a retrograde turn; but fortunately the important abatement of about 170*l.* in the port charges still continues.

Previously to 1825 foreigners had no legitimate mode of passing between Canton and Macao without paying irregular fees, to the amount of about 50*l.* on each trip, which was found so serious a grievance, that it was determined to make a vigorous effort to obtain its discontinuance.   Accordingly, after various petitions were presented, without effect, through the usual channel of the Hong merchants, thirty-seven foreigners (of whom the author was one), of different nations, resolved to rush into the city, to obtain an audience of the Viceroy. Not knowing his Excellency's residence, however, they entered the first official dwelling which came in their way, and which chanced to be that of the Kwang-Hee, an officer in charge of the police.   Here, after a time, they were met by the Hong merchants, who used every persuasion and artifice to induce them to retire, while the Mandarins were collecting troops to surround and intimidate them.   All, however, in vain !   At last, as the dusk of the evening approached, the Chinese, seeing no other mode of dislodging the intruders, gave a pledge (which has ever since been rigidly kept), that the objectionable fees should be discontinued; and the invaders of Canton walked quietly home! Next day an edict was published, alleging that each of these foreigners had been tied to a soldier's back, and so carried out of the city, to be placed in custody of the Hong merchants, *there to await the punishment due to so heinous an offence.* On this occasion the presiding Mandarin passed his hand round the author's neck, to intimate that he would lose his head if he should ever venture on a repetition of so audacious a proceeding.

In 1807 and 1821 serious discussions and interruptions of trade occurred, in consequence of the Chinese demanding the surrender of Englishmen, to suffer death in retaliation for the loss of the lives of natives in affrays with English sailors. On both occasions the firmness of the supercargoes induced the Chinese to *desist from their demands,* contrary to the fatal precedent afforded by the sacrifice of the gunner of the Lady Hughes, who was unceremoniously strangled in 1784. Sir James Urmston, chief of the factory in 1821, received the honour of knighthood for the judiciousness of his negotiations.

But, a more remarkable instance than either

(already recorded in these pages*) occurred in 1833, when the Chinese, being unable to obtain the surrender of a British victim, actually *hired a foreigner to personate the alleged guilty individual, and undergo the farce of a trial, under a pledge of his life being spared!*

REMARKABLE IMPERIAL EDICT,

Reprehending the extortions of the Hong Merchants, issued at the close of the discussions with Lord Napier.

" At Canton there are merchants who have of late been in the habit of levying private duties, and incurring debts to barbarians; and it is requested that regulations be established to eradicate utterly such misdemeanors. The commercial intercourse of outside barbarians with the inner land is owing indeed, to the compassion of the celestial empire. If all the duties which are required to be paid can, indeed, be levied according to the fixed tariff, the said barbarian merchants must certainly pay them gladly, and must continually remain tranquil. *But if, as is now reported, the Hong merchants*

---

* See note, p. 64.

have of late been in a feeble and deficient state, and have, in addition to the government duties, added also private duties; while fraudulent individuals have further taken advantage of this to make gain out of the Custom-house duties, peeling off (from the barbarians) layer after layer, and having gone also to the extreme degree of the government merchants, incurring debts to the barbarians, heaping thousands upon ten thousands; *whereby are stirred up sanguinary quarrels; if the merchants thus falsely, and under the name of tariff duties, extort each according to his own wishes,* going even to the extreme degree of incurring debts, amount upon amount, it is *not matter of surprise if the said barbarian merchants, unable to bear their grasping, stir up disturbance.* Thus, with regard to the affair this year of the English Lord Napier, and others, disobeying the national laws and bringing forces into the inner river, the barbarians being naturally crafty and artful, and gain being their only object, we have no assurance that it was not owing to the numerous extortions of the Canton native merchants, that they, their minds being discontented, thereupon craftily thought to carry themselves with a high hand.   If regulations be not plainly established, strictly prohibiting these things, how can the barbarous multitude be kept in subjection, and misdemeanors be eradicated ?

" Let Loo (the Governor) and his colleagues examine with sincerity and earnestness; and if offences of the above description exist, let them immediately inflict severe punishment; therefore let there not be the least connivance or screening.   Let them also, with their whole hearts, consult and deliberate; and report fully and with fidelity as to the measures they, on investigation, propose for the secure establishment of regulations; so as to create confident hopes that the barbarians will be disposed to submit gladly, and that fraudulent merchants will not dare to indulge in peeling and scraping them.   Then will they (Loo and his colleagues) not fail of fulfilling the duties of their offices. Make known this edict.   Respect this."

ON THE ARBITRARY DUTIES LEVIED ON
FOREIGN TRADE AT CANTON.

Partly abstracted from a paper of the East India Company's Factory.

" The impossibility of obtaining from the Government any fixed tariff of duties, has been for many years one of the prominent evils in the commercial system of Canton; and it being the policy of all parties, Government, Hong merchants, and Linguists, to keep foreigners in a perfect state of ignorance of the mode and rate of duties levied on foreign trade, this may in a great measure account for the circumstance, that scarcely any two persons who have endeavoured to gain information on these points, could arrive at the same result." An official Custom House book for the province of Canton, has been printed by Imperial authority in five volumes, which, however, is but rarely procurable by foreigners, and only with considerable difficulty and expense. This contains the tariff which ought to regulate the payment of duties. In addition to the prescribed rates, it directs a further charge of 11⅔ per cent. on the amount of duty; in lieu of which, however, the Canton Custom-house levies 30 per cent., being an unauthorised increase of nearly a fifth; while ·15 decimals of a tael, per pecul, are charged for weighing expenses in lieu of only ·038 decimals, the prescribed rate. But these are relatively unimportant in comparison with the heavy exaction of 3 per cent., which the Hong merchants unauthorisedly levy on all goods, excepting woollens, long cloths, cotton yarn, and iron, as a contribution to what is called the CONSOO FUND, originally instituted for the purpose of liquidating the foreign debts of bankrupt Hong merchants;* but never honestly

---

* See *ante*, page 96.

appropriated to that object. And the Cohong having lately passed a new regulation disclaiming their *corporate* liability for such debts, no legitimate plea remains for the continuance of this irregular imposition; which ought not to be longer submitted to. Thus diverted from its original purpose, the Consoo fund is now appropriated, by the Hong merchants, solely to bribery and to the payment of the irregular exactions of the Mandarins (locally termed *squeezes*). The annual amount thus wrung from foreign traders, by the mere *fiat* of the Hong merchants, and entirely subject to their irresponsible control, is immense. The following are said to be some of the purposes to which it is appropriated :—

Annual tribute to the Emperor . . .	£18,000
For repairing the Yellow River embankments .	10,000
Expenses of an agent at Pekin . . .	7,000
Birth-day presents to the Emperor . . .	43,000
Do. do. to the Hoppo or Commissioner of Customs	7,000
Presents to do.'s mother or wife	7,000
Do. to various officers	13,000
Expenditure for Tartarian ginseng, which the Emperor compels them to purchase . . .	47,000
Total	£152,000

There is, however, yet another class of

charges to which foreign trade is liable, called *sze le*, business or trade regulations, which it is impossible to fix. " This consists entirely of an arrangement between the Hong merchant who acts as broker, and the native merchants who purchase the various articles; and varies according to the prices of the goods, and the expectations of those who profit by the charge. On some articles, particularly cotton and cotton twist, the amount is very considerable, comprising a great variety of charges, as allowance for loss of interest, different modes of payment, warehouse rent, expenses of weighing at Whampoa, &c.,—all these are expressed by distinct, and (to use a vulgar expression) slang terms, which are only intelligible to those Chinese who are intimately conversant with the particular trade to which they allude. In cotton, for instance, if sold at ten taels, only nine taels and seven decimals are paid, and the dollar is estimated at ·707, instead of ·718 decimals of a tael. What the object in this species of self-deception as to the nominal price is, it is difficult to say; but it really in some degree bears the appearance of being intended to mystify the transactions, so as to render them unintelligible to foreigners."

The bearing of the foregoing various charges

on the article of cotton is subjoined, by way of example : —

Authorized by Chinese Tariff.	Hong Merchants' Exactions.
COTTON, DECLS.	DECLS.
Imperial duty, tael 0·1500	.... tael 0·150
Authorized addition,	Hong Merchants' charge
11¾ per cent. ... 0·0174	30 per cent. .... 0·045
Do. weighing charge 0·0380	Ditto, ditto.......... 0·150
	Charged by the Hong
Authorized duty, tael 0·2054	Merchants, tael .... 0·345
	Add Consoo fund, 3 p. ct. 0·240
	Sze le, or trade charges 0·915

Total deduction, which a foreigner pays, from the price of his Cotton, per pecul........ } Tael 1·500

ON THE CRIMINAL AND ADMIRALTY JURISDICTION FOR THE TRIAL OF BRITISH SUBJECTS IN CHINA, CONFERRED, BY ACT OF PARLIAMENT, ON HIS MAJESTY'S SUPERINTENDENTS.

This anomalous jurisdiction has been denounced by many as an unjustifiable *imperium in imperio,* which could not possibly be tolerated by the Chinese with any regard to their independence as a nation. This, however, is very far from being the case; and the jurisdiction in question formed no part of the grounds on which the Chinese objected to receive the late

Lord Napier. "Of late years," says Dr. Morrison, "the plan adopted by the Chinese, in cases of homicide, has been to demand of the fellow-countrymen of the alleged manslayer, that the guilty person should be found out, and handed over to the Chinese for punishment. This is in effect to constitute them a criminal court. Were a man to be delivered up by the individuals thus called upon, he would be regarded by the government as already condemned. His punishment, painful experience tells us, would be certain. Since, then, the Chinese are thus ready to regard foreigners as the judges of their fellow-countrymen, why should foreign governments hesitate to establish criminal courts ?" *

Repeated government edicts might be quoted in support of these views. Let one suffice— issued on the occasion of the American homicide, in 1821 :—

" As the officers of government do not understand the language of the foreigners, it has always heretofore been the practice to order the chiefs of the respective countries to find out the murderer, and question him fully, and ascertain distinctly the facts, and then deliver him up to government; after which a Linguist is sum-

---

* From a paper by the late Dr. Morrison, in his son's Commercial Guide, p. 61.

moned, the interrogatories translated, and the evidence written down, and the prosecution conducted to a close."

The representatives of Christian powers in Turkey have long exercised a nearly similar jurisdiction. "For very many years," it is stated in M'Farlane's Constantinople, "no such thing as an execution of Franks, by Turkish law, had been seen in the Levant, where offenders are given over to their respective consuls, who take into their own hands their punishment, if the offence be light, or send them home to be tried by the laws of their country, if serious."

REMARKS ON HOMICIDES IN CHINA,

By the late Rev. Dr. R. Morrison.

"From what foreigners have witnessed in cases of manslaughter, they have inferred that the Chinese government acted rather from a spirit of revenge than according to law. That this is true appears to be indeed the case from a state paper quoted in the 34th section of the Chinese penal code. During the 11th moon of the 13th year of Keënlung, A. D. 1749, the then governor of Canton, named Yĕseun, reported to the Emperor, that he had tried *Aooloo* and other Macao foreigners, who had caused the death of two Chinese;* and having sentenced them to be bastinaded and transported, had to request that, according to foreign laws, they might be sent to Demaun. To this the Emperor replied, that the governor had managed very erroneously; that he should have required ' life for life.'—' If,' it was added, ' you quote only our native laws, and according to them sentence to the bastinado and transportation, then the fierce and unruly dispositions of the foreigners will cease to be afraid.' The Emperor thus declared (and his imperial decision is reprinted with every new edition of the laws), that the *native law* alone is *not* to be the guide of the local government when the foreigners cause the death of natives.— *Tsze ying yih ming yih te*—' it is incumbent to have life for life,'—in order to frighten and repress the barbarians.

" The Emperor was wroth with the governor for transporting the criminals to Demaun; and directed that, if not yet sent away, the sentence should be reversed and death inflicted. If already gone, a proclamation was to be issued to the foreigners, telling them that the mode of treatment would be different hereafter,

---

* The European account is, that two soldiers murdered two Chinese, and were falsely represented insane.

that so foreigners might all fear and obey. By sending the men to Demaun, said his Majesty, it became uncertain to the Chinese whether they received any punishment or not. The lost lives of the two natives were therefore considered not worth a straw.

" From this account it is evident that foreigners do not enjoy the protection of the Chinese laws. For them there is but one rule in all cases—life for life. For the Chinese, on the contrary, there are these three distinctions :

" 1. Killing with intention,—punishable by death.

" 2. Killing by pure accident,—a mulctuary offence.

"3. Killing in lawful self-defence,—not punishable at all.

"The first, indeed—killing with intention,—is more comprehensive than in the west, including all deaths occasioned, however remotely, by affrays, or dangerous sports;—thus if a bystander is killed by a blow aimed at another, in anger or in sport, it is reckoned intentional murder, and usually punished by death; though in a modified form. Purely accidental manslaughter is that caused by something beyond the control of the manslayer, as the dropping of a stone, hatchet, &c. which by chance falls on and kills a passer-by. Killing in self-defence is much more restricted than with us."

MEMORIALS

TO HIS MAJESTY'S GOVERNMENT,

SOLICITING PROTECTION TO THE BRITISH TRADE IN CHINA,

FROM THE MERCHANTS OF

MANCHESTER, LIVERPOOL, GLASGOW, AND CANTON.

To the Right Honourable The Lord Viscount Melbourne,
First Commissioner of His Majesty's Treasury, &c.
and

The Right Honourable The Lord Viscount Palmerston, M.P.
His Majesty's Secretary of State for Foreign Affairs,
&c. &c.

The Memorial of the President, Vice President, and Directors
of the Chamber of Commerce and Manufactures at
Manchester,

SHEWETH,

That your memorialists beg to draw your Lordships
attention to the great importance of the trade to China, to
the mercantile, manufacturing, and shipping interests of
Great Britain, and to the unprotected situation of our com-

merce in that country, and of our fellow-subjects resident in China, through whose medium the trade is conducted.

That the trade appears to your memorialists, to be capable of great extension and of increased advantages to this country. Its present importance may be briefly brought to your Lordships notice.

It affords employment for nearly one hundred thousand tons of British shipping.

It affords a market for the manufactures of this country to a large and rapidly increasing amount, and for the productions of our Indian possessions, to the extent, it is believed, of upwards of three millions sterling per annum, which enables our Indian subjects to consume our manufactures on a largely increased scale.

That no country presents to us the basis of a more legitimate and mutually advantageous trade than China; for the productions of that country, are as admirably suited to our wants and necessities, as ours are to theirs. The returns which China present to us, for these large imports from Great Britain and India, are principally teas and raw silk. That the value of raw silk imported from China, exceeds one million of pounds sterling per annum, the want of which would greatly paralyze a most important and rapidly growing manufacture.

That your memorialists cannot contemplate without the most serious alarm, the uncertain and unprotected state, in which this most important trade is placed, more particularly since the failure of the late Lord Napier's mission.

That this large and valuable trade, is at the present moment without any adequate protection, and subjected to the arbitrary exactions of the Hong merchants, (a body of men through whom alone our transactions are permitted to be conducted, nearly all of them in embarrassed circumstances, and many of them insolvent,) and of the corrupt local officers at Canton, whose exactions, it is believed, are contrary to the law of the Empire, and to the wishes of the government.

That the trade is liable at any moment to be stopped by the caprice of the Hong merchants and local government, whose exactions, beyond what the law authorizes, are frequent.

That British property is daily in jeopardy; our countrymen daily subjected to insult; our Sovereign, in the person of His Representative, the late Lord Napier, has been subjected to indignity; our industry is liable to be paralyzed; our revenue exposed to the loss of from four to five millions sterling a-year. This accumulation of evils your memorialists beg most respectfully, but most earnestly to submit, calls for the protecting influence of the British Government, which, it is believed, will prove more effective, if directed to the supreme Government, than through the corrupt and distant medium of the inferior officers at Canton.

Your memorialists, therefore, humbly pray that your Lordships will take into your early and serious consideration, the nature of our political relations with China, and that your Lordships will adopt such measures, as, in your wisdom may be considered most effectual, for the protection of British subjects resident in China, and the property entrusted to their care.

And as in duty bound they will ever pray.

Manchester, February, 1836.

TO THE RIGHT HONOURABLE

THE LORD VISCOUNT MELBOURNE,

FIRST LORD OF HIS MAJESTY'S TREASURY :

THE MEMORIAL OF THE LIVERPOOL EAST INDIA ASSOCIATION,

RESPECTFULLY SHEWETH,

That your memorialists view, with serious uneasiness, the unprotected state in which the extensive trade between this country and China is placed, especially since the failure of the mission of the late Lord Napier.

This trade labours under two great evils, from which arise most of the other grievances by which it is oppressed :—First, the imposition, by the Canton local officers, of unauthorised and arbitrary duties, greatly exceeding the established tariff. And secondly, the restriction of the trade to ten or twelve Chinese, under the name of Hong merchants, most of whom are in embarrassed circumstances. To these Hong merchants all imports must be passed for sale, wholly out of the owner's custody and control, and while they thus monopolize the trade of British subjects, they are invested with the inconsistent power of governing them, under the plea that Europeans are a barbarous and degraded race, unfit to be placed within the pale of Chinese law, and therefore not to be allowed to approach the tribunals and established authorities of the country. Hence results a systematic denial of justice, accompanied by an endless train of wrongs and disabilities, which greatly hinder the natural progress of the trade, which they assume the right to suspend entirely at any moment, whenever they may be desirous of enforcing the submission of foreigners to their irregular proceedings. This power they recently exercised, as your Lordship is aware, by putting a stop to commercial dealings, on their own authority, without even the form of a government order, in the course of their discussions with the late Lord Napier, on the mere ground of his Lordship's residing in Canton; a proceeding which it is important to distinguish from the more serious events which followed on His Majesty's ships returning the fire of the Chinese forts when on their progress to join the merchant shipping, at Whampoa.

Should the indignities offered to His Majesty's representative, terminating in his Lordship's death, and the severe losses occasioned to British merchants and ship owners, from the stoppage of trade which then occurred, be allowed to pass without effectual remonstrance on the part of His Majesty's government, your memorialists apprehend not only a material aggravation of existing evils, but the strongest probability of constant collisions and interruptions of trade, equally prejudicial to British merchants, as to the immense revenue derivable from that source to His Majesty's Exchequer.

From the professions of good will towards foreigners, uniformly expressed in Imperial edicts, and the redress afforded in the rare instances in which an appeal to the supreme government was formerly practicable, your memorialists are impressed with the conviction that the grievances under which the trade is suffering, are attributable, rather to the corrupt administration of the Canton local officers, than to any adverse feeling on the part of the Imperial cabinet.

Your memorialists will only add, that the trade for which they thus solicit protection, employs about six millions sterling of British capital, and ninety thousand tons of shipping, besides yielding an annual revenue of four to five millions sterling, on the single commodity of tea; while it supplies to a great extent the article of raw silk, now become indispensable to a rising and important branch of British manufactures.

Your memorialists, therefore, earnestly pray, that your Lordship will adopt such measures as may secure for British commerce and British subjects in China, the same degree of protection, which His Majesty's government extends to them in other foreign countries.

Liverpool, February, 1836.

(COPY.)

UNTO THE

RIGHT HON. LORD VISCOUNT MELBOURNE,

FIRST LORD OF HIS MAJESTY'S TREASURY, &c. &c. &c.

THE MEMORIAL OF THE GLASGOW EAST INDIA
ASSOCIATION,

RESPECTFULLY SHEWETH,

That while your memorialists feel deeply sensible of the value of that great measure of parliament, by which the China seas were opened to the enterprise of the British nation, they feel themselves called upon to represent to your Lordship the importance of having the trade with China placed on a more secure footing than it at present enjoys.

Your memorialists lament the unfortunate result of the late Lord Napier's mission to China, by which the position of Great Britain with that country has not been improved. Now, as formerly, personal liberty is quite insecure, and the British merchant possesses no kind of control over the sale or realization of his own property. The goods of British traders must be passed for sale wholly out of the hands of the owner into those of the Hong merchants, upon whom the owner possesses no check whatever. The trade is subjected to numerous duties and heavy exactions, the rate and the mode of charging which are arbitrary, and for the payment of a large proportion of which the Hong merchants are held responsible by the Chinese government, thus placing in jeopardy the whole property of British subjects and others, for debts due to government by these Hong merchants, the majority of whom it is notorious are in arrears for years past, and are in an insolvent state.

These and other grievances will prevent the free trade of Great Britain and China from expanding itself with the rapidity and to the extent which the immense scope afforded by the latter country, and the liberty lately granted by the British legislature, would otherwise not fail to induce.

Your memorialists therefore submit to your Lordship, that it would be of incalculable benefit to this country and our Indian possessions, were it practicable to devise means for establishing such a treaty of amity and commerce as would remove the disadvantages under which the trade at present labours; including also, if possible, a restoration of the privilege formerly possessed of trading to Amoy and other ports on the east coast of China.

While your memorialists forbear recommending any particular method of attaining this end, surrounded as the question is with much difficulty, they cannot omit stating to your Lordship, that in their opinion the object intended is much

more likely to be accomplished by a direct application to the
court at Pekin, than by negotiation through inferior officers of
the Chinese government.

Your memorialists presume further to suggest to your Lordship, that failing a satisfactory arrangement with the Chinese
government, it would be of the greatest advantage to British
trade in that part of the world, were his Majesty's government
to obtain one or more of the islands near to China, as an em-
porium for carrying on commerce free from the exactions,
control, or annoyance of the Chinese government. In the
conviction that this important subject will receive due consideration from your Lordship, the memorialists, as in duty
bound, will ever pray.

Signed on behalf of the East India Association of the City
of Glasgow,

(Signed)   KIRKMAN FINLAY, Chairman.

2nd June, 1835.

TO THE

KING'S MOST EXCELLENT MAJESTY

IN COUNCIL:

THE PETITION OF THE UNDERMENTIONED BRITISH
SUBJECTS AT CANTON,

HUMBLY SHEWETH,

That we are induced, by the extraordinary position in which we feel ourselves placed in relation to the Chinese government, to petition your Majesty in council to take such measures as may be adapted alike to maintain the honour of our country, and the advantages which a safe and uninterrupted commerce with China is calculated to yield to the revenues of Great Britain, and to the important classes interested in its arts and manufactures. *The extraordinary state of our relations with the Chinese induces us to petition your Majesty.*

We beg humbly to represent, that at the present moment, the commissioners appointed by your Majesty to superintend the affairs of British subjects trading at Canton, are not acknowledged by the constituted authorities of this country, and that they are not permitted to reside within the limits to which their jurisdiction is, by their commission, strictly confined; while they are forbidden by their instructions to appeal to the imperial government at Peking, and are perfectly powerless to resent the indignities offered to the late chief superintendent, or to compel reparation for the injuries done *Your Majesty's superintendents are prohibited by the Chinese from exercising their functions: and are not empowered by your Majesty to appeal to Peking.*

K

to your Majesty's subjects by the late unprovoked stoppage of their trade.

Your petitioners are well persuaded that the powers vested in your Majesty's commissioners were thus restricted with the express object of avoiding, as far as possible, all occasion of collision with the Chinese authorities; while it was hoped that, by maintaining a direct intercourse with the principal officers of government, instead of indirectly communicating through the Hong merchants, a sure way would be opened for the improvement of the present very objectionable footing on which foreign merchants stand in this country, and for security against the many wrongs and inconveniences which they have had to suffer in the present state of their commercial avocations.

The whole history of intercourse with China proves that the most unsafe of all courses in treating with its government is that of submission to contempt or wrongs. Your petitioners, however, beg leave most earnestly to submit to your Majesty in council, their thorough conviction, founded on the invariable tenor of the whole history of foreign intercourse with China, as well as of its policy on occasions of internal commotion, down to the present moment, that the most unsafe of all courses that can be followed in treating with the Chinese government, or any of its functionaries, is that of quiet submission to insult, or such unresisting endurance of contemptuous or wrongful treatment, as may compromise the honour, or bring into question the power of our country. We cannot, therefore, but deeply deplore that such authority to negotiate, and such force to protect from insult, as the occasion demands, were not entrusted to your Majesty's commissioners, confident as we are, without a

If Lord Napier had been furnished with force and authority to resent insult, we are confident, without a shadow of doubt, that his mission would have succeeded. shadow of doubt, that, had the requisite powers, properly sustained by an armed force, been possessed by your Majesty's late first commissioner, the lamented Lord Napier, we should not now have to deplore the degraded and insecure position in which we are placed, in consequence of the representative of our Sovereign having been compelled to retire from Canton, without having authority to offer any remonstrance to the supreme government, or to make a demonstration of a resolution to obtain reparation at once, for the insults wantonly heaped upon him by the local authorities.

Your petitioners, therefore, humbly pray that your Majesty will be pleased to grant powers plenipotentiary to such person of suitable rank, discretion, and diplomatic experience, as your Majesty, in your wisdom may think fit and proper to be entrusted with such authority; and your petitioners would suggest that he be directed to proceed to a convenient station on the east coast of China, as near to the capital of the country as may be found most expedient, in one of your Majesty's ships of the line, attended by a sufficient maritime force, which we are of opinion need not consist of more than two frigates, and three or four armed vessels of light draft, together with a steam vessel, all fully manned; that he may, previously to landing, require, in the first instance, in the name of your Majesty, ample reparation for the insults offered by the governor of Kwangtung and Kwangse in his edicts published on the occasion of Lord Napier's arrival at Canton, and the subsequent humiliating conduct pursued towards his Lordship, to which the aggravation of his illness and death may be attributed; as well as for the arrogant and degrading language used towards your Majesty and our country in edicts emanating from the local authorities, wherein your Majesty was represented as the " reverently submissive" tributary of the Emperor of China, and your Majesty's subjects as profligate barbarians, and that they be retracted, and never again employed by Chinese functionaries : that he may also demand reparation for the insult offered to your Majesty's flag by firing on your Majesty's ships of war from the forts at the Bogue, and that remuneration shall be made to your Majesty's subjects for the losses they have sustained by the detention of their ships during the stoppage of their trade. After these preliminaries shall have been conceded, (as your petitioners have no doubt they will be,) and not till then, your petitioners humbly suggest that it will be expedient for your Majesty's plenipotentiary to propose the appointment of com-

Marginal notes:

We pray your Majesty to grant powers plenipotentiary to an officer of diplomatic experience to proceed to China in a ship of the line, with two frigates, sloops, and a steamer;

to require reparation for insults and wrongs to Lord Napier, terminating in that nobleman's death; for firing on your Majesty's ships, and for offensive edicts representing your Majesty as a " reverently submissive" tributary, and your subjects as profligate barbarians; also remuneration for losses arising from stoppage of trade:

thereafter to propose mutually beneficial arrangements; in agreeing to which we do not anticipate difficulty.

R 2

missioners on the part of the Chinese government, to adjust
with him, on shore, such measures as may be deemed most
effectual to the prevention of future occasion of complaint and
misunderstanding, and for the promotion and extension of
the trade generally, to the mutual advantage of both countries.
Your petitioners believe, that if these matters shall be fairly
represented, so as to do away with all reasonable objection,
and the favourable inclination of the Chinese commissioners
be gained, there will be found little disposition on the part of
the supreme government to withhold its assent, and every
desirable object will thus have been attained.

nor risk of inter-
rupti n to the
Canton trade,
Your petitioners would humbly entreat your Majesty's
favourable view of these suggestions, in the confidence that
they may be acted upon, not only with every prospect of
success, but without the slightest danger to the existing com-
as the force re-
commended
would enable the
plenipotentiary
to secure in-
demnity for
wrongs, by repri-
sals on the
Chinese trade,
and by intercept-
ing the imperial
revenues in tran-
situ ; should such
measures be ne-
cessary:
mercial intercourse, inasmuch, as even with a force not exceeding that which we have proposed should be placed at the
disposal of your Majesty's plenipotentiary, there would be no
difficulty, should proceedings of a compulsory nature be required, in putting a stop to the greater part of the external
and internal commerce of the Chinese empire ;—in intercepting its revenues in their progress to the capital, and in taking
possession of all the armed vessels of the country. Such
measures would not only be sufficient to evince both the
power and spirit of Great Britain to resent insult, but would
enable your Majesty's plenipotentiary to secure indemnity for
any injury that might, in the first instance, be offered to the
persons or property of your Majesty's subjects ; and would
speedily induce the Chinese government to submit to just and
reasonable terms. We are, at the same time, confident, that
resort even to such measures as these, so far from being likely
which we anx-
iously wish to
avoid.
to lead to more serious warfare, an issue which both our
interests and inclinations alike prompt us to deprecate, would
be the surest course for avoiding the danger of such a collision.

Re-admission to
the ports for-
merly open,
Amoy, &c.,
Your petitioners beg to submit that the mere restoration of
the liberty once possessed of trading to Amoy, Ningpo, and

Chusan, would be followed by the most beneficial conse-quences, not merely in the more extended field thereby opened for commercial enterprise, but in the rivalry which would be excited as formerly, in the officers of government at these several ports, to attract the resort of foreign merchants, and thus extend their own opportunities of acquiring emoluments from the trade.

would be benefi-cial in reviving competition.

With respect, however, to this point, or any other of com-mercial interest that it would be expedient to make the sub-ject of negotiation, your petitioners would humbly suggest that your Majesty's minister in China should be instructed to put himself in communication with the merchants of Canton, qualified as they must be in a certain degree by their expe-rience and observation to point out, in what respect the bene-fits that might be reaped under a well regulated system of commercial intercourse, are curtailed or lost in consequence of the restrictions to which the trade is at present subjected, and the arbitrary and irregular exactions to which it is ex-posed either directly, or not less severely because indirectly, through the medium of the very limited number of merchants licensed to deal with foreigners. As an instance of the latter, your petitioners may state the fact, that the whole expense of the immense preparations lately made by the local govern-ment to oppose the expected advance towards Canton of your Majesty's frigates after they had passed the Bogue, has been extorted from the Hong merchants ; and as but a few of them are in a really solvent state, they have no other means of meeting this demand, but by combining to tax both the import and export trade.

On all points of commercial grievance, it will be desirable that the plenipoten-tiary apply for information to the British mer-chants at Canton.

We would further humbly, but urgently, submit, that as we cannot but trace the disabilities and restrictions under which our commerce now labours, to a long acquiescence in the ar-rogant assumption of supremacy over the monarchs and people of other countries, claimed by the Emperor of China for himself and his subjects, we are forced to conclude that no essentially beneficial result can be expected to arise out of

To acquiescence in the supremacy claimed by the Chinese over other nations, we trace existing disa-bilities; nor while this continues do we think relief attainable.

negotiations, in which such pretensions are not decidedly repelled. We most seriously apprehend, indeed, that the least
concession or waving of this point under present circumstances, could not fail to leave us as much as ever subject
to a repetition of the injuries of which we have now to
complain.

We would, therefore, humbly beseech your Majesty not to
be induced by a paternal regard for your subjects trading to
this remote empire, to leave it to the discretion of any future
representative of your Majesty, as was permitted in the case
of the embassy of Lord Amherst, to swerve in the smallest
degree from a direct course of calm and dispassionate, but
determined maintenance of the true rank of your Majesty's
empire in the scale of nations, well assured as we feel, that
any descent from such just position, would be attended with
worse consequences than if past events were to remain un-
noticed, and we were to be left for the future to conduct our
concerns with the Chinese functionaries, each as he best
may.

It would ill become your Majesty's petitioners to point to
any individual as more competent than another to undertake
the office of placing on a secure and advantageous footing
our commercial relations with this country. We may, however, perhaps be permitted to suggest the inexpediency of
assigning such a task to any person previously known in
China as connected with commerce conducted under the
trammels and degradations to which it has hitherto been
subjected, or to any one, in short, who has had the misfor-
tune either in a public or private capacity, to endure insult or
injury from Chinese authorities.

Equally inexpedient would it be, as appears to your petitioners, to treat with any functionary not specially nominated
by the Imperial cabinet, and not on any account with those
of Canton, whose constant course of corrupt and oppressive
conduct forms a prominent ground of complaint; or to permit any future commissioner to set his foot on the shores of

[Marginal note beside second paragraph:] We pray that your Majesty will not make any conces- sion on this point, preferring, as we do, that your Ma- jesty, rather than acknowledge Chi- nese supremacy, should leave us to our own resources.

[Marginal note beside third paragraph:] We pray that no persons who have been engaged here in trade, or who have submitted to indignities from the Chinese, be employed to ne- gotiate; that only functionaries ac- credited from Peking be ne- gotiated with, not those of Canton, and that no Bri- tish commissioner shall land till as- sured of a becom- ing reception.

China, until ample assurance is afforded of a reception and treatment suitable to the dignity of a minister of your Majesty, and the honour of an empire that acknowledges no superior on earth.

And your petitioners shall ever pray, &c.

Canton, 9th December, 1834.

[Signed by thirty-five of about forty-five individuals, composing the resident British trading community, by all the commanders of the East India Company's ships who revisited Canton after the opening of the trade, and by several other commanders and traders,—making in all eighty-eight signatures.]

ON ACCOUNT OF THE HONOURABLE COMPANY.

						Taels.	Dollars.
Broad cloth ....Bales	6,652	Yds.	687,914	..		704,743	
Long ells .... "	7,525	Pcs.	150,186	..		765,799	
Camlets ....: .... "	450	"	4,500	..		61,176	
British Cotton piece goods .... "	1,220	"	30,500	..		127,260	
Ditto Cotton twist .... "	1,000	Peculs	1,800	..		66,090	
Ditto Stuffs, Union satinets, and Chintzes (experimental)						4,806	
Ditto Iron ....Tons	1,202	Peculs	20,202	..		23,273	
Lead .... "	1,110	"	18,655	..		57,830	
					Taels.		
Cotton, Bengal ....Bales 23,824		"	53,719	..	628,507	1,810,977	
" Bombay .... " 21,978		"	62,528	..	697,972		
						1,326,479	
Ebony ....Logs	823	"	141	..		54	
						3,137,510	4,357,653

ON PRIVATE ACCOUNT.

		T. M.	Taels.		
Cotton, Bengal ....Peculs 43,751	a	11 7 p. pecul	511,887		
" Madras .... "	4,229	' 12 7 "	53,708		
" Bombay .... "	278,413	' 10 6 "	2,951,178	3,516,773	4,884.407

		Dols.	Dollars.		
Opium, Patna and Benares......Chests 7,511	' 639 p. chs.	4,799,529			
" Malwa ....,...... " 10,102½	' 675 "	6,819,187	Dollars.		
			11,618,716		
" 17,613½					

		Dols.		
Sandal wood...............Peculs 3,680	a 11¼ p. pecul	..	41,400	
Pepper .... " 23,122	' 8¼ "	..	190.757	
Rattans .... " 13,052	' 3 "	..	39,156	
Betel nut .... " 57,025	' 2½ "	..	142,562	
Putchuck .... " 2,105	' 13½ "	..	28,417	
Olibanum .... " 4,444	' 4 "	..	17,776	
Ebony .... " 2,634	' 3 "	..	7,902	
Broad cloth ....Pieces 9,574	' 28 p. piece	..	268,072	
Long ells .... " 9,600	' 10½ "	..	100,800	
Worleys .... " 639	' 12 "	..	7,668	
Camlets .... " 571	' 23½ "	..	13,418	
Cotton piece goods........... " 45,422	' 4¾ "	..	215,754	
Printed ditto ....Value......	......	..	82,443	
Cotton twist .... Peculs 1,344	' 40 p. pecul	..	53,760	
Cochineal .... " 42	' 340 "	..	14,280	
Lead...................... " 3,893	' 4 "	..	15,572	
Steel .....,.............. " 1,486	' 4¾ "	..	7,058	
	Carriea forward		12,865,511	9,242,060

ON ACCOUNT OF THE HONOURABLE COMPANY.

			Taels.	Dollars.
Bohea ....Peculs 62,488 .... Taels	989,526			
Congo .... " 109,177 .... "	2,814,810			
Souchong .... " 3,370 .... "	127,462			
Peko..................... " 237 .... "	11,595			
Twankay .... " 29,781 .... "	812,474			
Hyson .... " 6,739 .... "	343,904			
Hyson Skin .... " 812 .... "	22,243			

	Taels.	Dollars.
	5,122,014	
North American Investment (Commission included)..Taels 366,356		
Cape and St. Helena Stores .... " 20,345		
Stores to Bengal, Madras, and Bombay............ " 12,328		
	399,029	
Bullion (Charges of Shipment included)...... Dls. 155,030 ..	111,622	
Port Charges on 24 Ships .... " 89,920		
Unloading Charges, Canton Factory Expenses, &c. 101,612	191,532	
	5,824,197	8,089,163

Viz.—Unloading Charges ....Taels 11,209
Factory Expenses............ " 65,055
Canton European Establishment " 5,776
H. C. Sloop................ " 2,996
Printing Establishment ...... " 989
Charges on Merchandize...... " 12,215
Charges extraordinary........ " 3,372

Taels 101,612

ON PRIVATE ACCOUNT.

	Ts.	Taels.	Taels.
Congo and Caper Congo ......Peculs 9,089 a 21 per pecul	190,869		
Souchong and Pouchong ...... " 1,468 ' 22 " "	32,296		
Peko and Orange Peko........ " 3,149 ' 29 " "	92,321		
Hyson .... " 124 ' 47 " "	5,828		
Gunpowder and Imperial ...... " 253 ' 55 " "	13,915		
		335,229	
Black Tea .... " 3,739	92,184		
Green Tea .... " 11,209	324,689	416,873	
Peculs 29,031		752,102	1,044,586

	Dols.	Dollars.	Dollars.
Raw Silk, Nankin.... .... " 8,061 a 332 " "	2,676,252		
" Canton............. " 1,418 ' 276 " "	391,368		
" Do. 5th sort........ " 441 ' 67 " "	29,547		
		3,097,167	
Nankeen Cloth.............. Pieces 30,600 ' 74 per 100 pieces	22,644		
Silk Piece Goods .... Value	332,844		
Sugar Candy................Peculs 10,734 ' 11 per pecul ..	118,074		
Soft Sugar................ " 17,705 ' 8¼ " " ..	146,066		
Cassia Lignea .... " 17,607 ' 8¼ " " ..	145,258		
Tortoiseshell and Scraps ......Value	7,822		
Mother o' pearl Shells .... " 2,049 ' 16¾ "	34,321		

	Taels.	Dollars.
Carried forward	3,904,196	9,133,749

					Dollars.	Dollars.
			Brought forward		12,865,511	9,242,060
Iron .... Peculs 9,735	*a*	*Ds.* 2.70	per pecul	..	26,285	
Tin	,, 5,762 ,	16	,,	..	92,192	
Smalts	,, 325 ,	77	,,	..	25,025	
Watches,Clocks,val.*Ds.*50,713 . Glassware, Val. *Ds.*12,508					63,221	
Coral beads	,, 18,480 . Amber	,,	5,000		23,480	
Skins .... Number 18,069		Value		..	17,306	
Pearls and Diamonds		,, ...		..	252,437	
Cornelians	......	,, ...		..	36,850	
Ivory and Ele- phant's teeth } Peculs 84		*Ds.* 74	per pecul	..	6,216	
Fish maws......	,, 1,472	56	,,	..	82,432	
Sharks' fins	,, 5,348	25	,,	..	133,700	
Birds' nests .... Catties 630		21	per catty	..	13,230	
Cow bezoar	,, 400	22	,,	..	8,800	
Camphor, Baroos	,, 426	24	,,	..	10,224	
Cloves .... Peculs 610		25	per pecul	..	15,250	
Nutmegs	,, 19	84	,,	..	1,596	
Saltpetre	,, 6,044	9	,,	..	54,396	
Rice	258,822	2·60	,,	..	412,937	
Sundries ...... Value		......		..	73,145	
Dollars........	......	......		..	20,500	
						14,234,733
					Dollars	23,476,793

Company's Bills on the Bengal Government.. *Dls* 3,174,110
Commander's Cotton Bonds   960,955

Dls. 4,135,065

	Dollars.	Dollars.
Brought forward	3,904,196	9,133,749
Vermilion .... Boxes 3,576 *a* 34 per box ...	121,584	
Camphor .... Peculs 2,430 , 22 per pecul ..	53,460	
Alum .... ,, 10,213 , 2 ,, ..	20,426	
Rhubarb .... ,, 434 , 58 ,, ..	25,172	
Aniseed Oil ...... ,, 20 , 165 ,, ..	3,300	
China-root, Gallangal, Gamboge and Musk .. Value ..	33,457	
Floor and Table Mats .... 28,691 .... ,, ..	13,055	
Bamboos and Whanghees.. .... ,, ..	14,389	
Pearls, False pearls & Glass-beads .... ,, ..	26,291	
China-ware .... ,, ..	13,525	
Paper Kittisols, Lacquered ware, Fire works ,,	106,543	
Brass-leaf .... Boxes 81 *a* 46 per box ..	3,726	
Cotton Piece Goods, Pieces 1,250 *a* 6 per piece ..	7,500	
Cotton Twist ..... Peculs 201 , 42 per pecul ..	8,442	
Cochineal .... ,, 202 , 218. ,, ..	44,036	
South American Copper ,, 10,907 , 20 ,, ..	218,140	
Sundries, viz. Gold, Silver, Ivory, and Tortoiseshell Ware, Sweetmeats, Pictures, &c.	115,694	
Silver Bullion (Sycee, South American Silver, and Dollars),	6,062,790	
Gold	513,795	
Disbursements on 20 Regular Ships *a* 12,000 *Ds.* 4 Chartered Ships at 4,000 *Ds.*, 20 Country Ships *a* 8,000, *Ds.* 16 Rice Ships at Whampoa, at 3,000 *Ds.* and 44 Ships at Lintin, at 1,500 *Ds.* each......................	———	11,309,521
	....	530,000
BALANCE	....	2,503,523
	Dollars	23,476,793

Tea, to England.	Company's.	Private Trade.
Black.............	lbs. 23,369,600....	lbs. 1,827,467
Green.............	4,977,600....	50,267
	lbs. 28,347,200....	lbs. 1,877,734

MACAO, 31st March, 1834.

EXPORT OF SILVER BULLION.

	Dollars.		Dollars.	Dollars.
To England :—Sp. and Brazil Dollars	128,739	—Mexican bar silver =	26,941	..155,730
Calcutta : ,, ,, ,,	104,704	—Sycee silver equal to	1,825,227	1,929,931
Bombay : ,, " "	671,633	— ,, ,,	3,182,647	3,854,280
Sundry places ,, ,, ,,	143,295	— ,, ,,	111,430	
		S. American silver—	23,154	277,879

Total Export of Bullion, the Company's included,   6,217,820

Note. Sycee silver valued at 2 per cent. premium, at 718 taels per 1,000 Dollars.

IMPORTS.

	Quantity.	Average Price.		TOTAL VAL. Sp. Dollars.
Broad Cloth............Pce.	22028	31·54	Pr Pce.	694829
Cotton Yarn ....Pls.	3850	40·44	Picul	145609
Scarlet Cuttings .... ,,	541	77·43	,,	41890
Cotton, Bengal........... ,,	136415	16·70	,,	2278992
Ditto, Bombay........... ,,	291770	16·40	,,	4789355
Ditto, Madras .... ,,	16889	16·33	,,	275900
Sandalwood .... ,,	3025	14·85	,,	44926
Pepper................ ,,	1972	7·34	,,	14476
Rattans................. ,,	18508	2·55	,,	46434
Rice................... ,,	288580	2·19	,,	623135
Betel Nut............... ,,	11601	2·92	,,	33963
Putchuck .... ,,	3224	8·27	,,	26666
Olibanum............... ,,	2593	3·11	,,	7985
Ivory and Elephant's Teeth.. ,,	132	52·65	,,	6950
Saltpetre................ ,,	3095	7·74	,,	23971
Oil.................... ,,	30	6·00	,,	180
Bicho de Mar............ ,,	156	12·69	,,	1981
Lead................... ,,	3713	4·68	,,	17379
Iron .... ,,	4473	1·95	,,	28346
Tin . ... ,,	2715	11·79	,,	32031
Steel.................. ,,	390	3·84	,,	1500
Spelter................ ,,	725	4·00	,,	2900
Smalts .... ,,	296	58·00	,,	17168
Copper................ ,,	171	32·11	,,	5472
Quicksilver .... ,,	1107	67·27	,,	74470
Flints .... ,,	5431	1·18	,,	8436
Tortoise-shell .... ,,	74	60·00	,,	4440
Cochineal.............. ,,	18	277·77	,.	5000
Ebony .... ,,	42	3·00	,,	126
Gambier .... ,,	97	3·00	,,	291
Coral Fragments.......... ,,	150	40·00	,,	6000
Fish Maws .... ,,	2482	49·88	,,	123833
Sharks' Fins............ ,,	3280	20·74	,,	68037
Mother O'Pearl Shells..... ,,	635	12·16	.,	7924
Cotton Piece Goods....... Pce.	11000	8·95	Piece	98460
Long ells .... ,,	66180	9·19	,,	608250
Camlets................ ,,	103	30·82	,,	3175
Chintzes .... ,,	2631	5·60	,,	14748
Cow Bezoar ....Cts.	327	23·00	Catty	7521
Amber .... ,,	6	11·00	,,	66
Woollens, various kinds..... Val.				12238
Pearls and Cornelians...... ,,				297707
Watches and Clocks........ ,,				11660
Glass Ware .... ,,				515
Dollars................ ,,				60000
Sundries .... ,,				157917
Opium Patna............Chs.	6245	576·75	Chest	3602045
Do. Benares .... ,,	1522	545·20	,,	829800
Do. Malwa............ ,,	8749	596·99	,,	5223125
				20387822
For East India Company's advances upon remittances at the rate of 4s. 7d. per Dollar..................				2231831
			Spanish Dollars	22,619,653

By order of the Superintendents of the Trade of British Subjects
From the Canton Press.

	Quantity.	Average Price.		TOTAL VAL. Sp. Dollars.
Black Tea .... Pls.	287287	29·15	Pr.Pls.	8374435
Green Tea .... ,,	70841	39·17	,,	2775239
Raw Silk Nanking .... ,,	4756	349·94	,,	1664326
Do. do. Canton .... ,,	2579	241·70	,,	623355
Sugar Candy .... ,,	17569	10·73	,,	188645
Soft Sugar .... ,,	31870	6·00	,,	191220
Cassia Lignea .... ,,	12864	9·17	,,	117986
Tortoise Shell .... ,,	35	57·14	,,	2000
Mother O'Pearl Shells ..... ,,	715	16·00	,,	11440
Camphor .... ,,	124	28·88	,,	36052
Alum .... ,,	15995	2·20	,,	35312
Rhubarb .... ,,	449	46·32	,,	20799
Dragon's Blood .... ,,	319	87·00	,,	27753
Aniseed Star .... ,,	65	11·76	,,	765
Coloured Paper, various sorts ,,	339	16·71	,,	5667
Cochineal .... ,,	209	224·79	,,	46983
Quicksilver .... ,,	98	65·40	,,	6410
Arsenic .... ,,	150	17·00	,,	2550
Copper .... ,,	3753	18·29	,,	68560
Iron .... ,,	500	1·95	,,	975
Tin .... ,,	112	16·00	,,	1792
Cubebs .... ,,	212	22·00	,,	4664
Indigo .... ,,	60	40·00	,,	2400
Glass Beads .... ,,	672	25·50	,,	17140
Nankin Cloth of all sorts.... Pce.	48003	1·36	Pce.	65331
Vermillion .... Box	1300	50·00	Box	65000
Brass Leaf .... ,,	290	48·53	,,	14095
Tobacco .... Case	300	17·66	Case	5300
Segars .... ,,	189	4·94	,,	935
Silk Piece Goods .... Val.				197684
Gold Jewels .... ,,				3858
Pearls .... ,,				11700
China root, Galg. and Musk.. ,,				10784
China Ware .... ,,				13165
Paper Kittis, and Lac. Ware ,,				60704
Dollars .... ,,				1036923
Sycee Silver .... ,,				2368511
Sundries .... ,,				158150
Marble Slabs .... ,,	4335	317·18	1000	1375
Bamboos and Whangees .... ,,	1560380	9·40	,,	14575
Gold in Taels Weight ...... ,,				554019
				18808577
Disbursements on 75 vessels at Whampoa, at *Dols.*8000 each..				600000
Ditto.......... 26 Rice do............		1500	,,	39000
Ditto.......... 46 vessels at Lintin.		1500	,,	69000
				19516577
Balance				3103076

38,304,933 lbs. or Pls. 287,287·00 of Black Tea
  9,445,467 ,,   ,,   70,841·01 Green do.

Total	47,750,400 lbs.	358,128·01 Piculs.
		Sp. Dols. 22,619,653

in China,

EDWARD EMSLIE, *Acting Secretary and Treasurer.*

www.ingramcontent.com/pod-product-compliance
Ingram Content Group UK Ltd.
Pitfield, Milton Keynes, MK11 3LW, UK
UKHW042152280225
455719UK00001B/281